AMERICAN PHILANTHROPY

American

THE CHICAGO HISTORY OF AMERICAN CIVILIZATION

Daniel J. Boorstin, EDITOR

Philanthropy

By Robert H. Bremner

 THE UNIVERSITY OF CHICAGO PRESS

Library of Congress Catalog Card Number: 60-7246

THE UNIVERSITY OF CHICAGO PRESS, CHICAGO & LONDON
The University of Toronto Press, Toronto 5, Canada

© *1960 by The University of Chicago. Published 1960*
Second Impression 1962
Printed in the U.S.A.

23838

Editor's Preface

We have long thought of ourselves immodestly as a nation of philanthropists. But in our generation American private philanthropy has dwarfed all our earlier good works, and the United States government has become a philanthropist on an unprecedented scale. Having cast ourselves in the role of a philanthropic nation—only to be blamed all over the world for the shortsightedness and selfishness of our good works— we should now try to discover precisely what our tradition has been.

Americans today need to understand the meaning of philanthropy and to see what is distinctive about our ways of doing good. Faithful Christians have often remarked that one of God's purposes in creating poverty was to make charity possible. In the United States, as Mr. Bremner shows in this volume, the emphasis has generally been quite different. One of God's purposes in creating American wealth, it is said, must have been to make philanthropy possible. Without great wealth, how could there be great philanthropy?

In this pioneering volume, Mr. Bremner gives us some much-needed help in defining our philanthropic tradition. He is neither a sentimentalist, a cynic, nor a muckraker. He is a ruthless and sympathetic historian. He does not suggest that Americans are by nature any more selfless or altruistic than other peoples. He does show how the peculiarly American situation has given a special character to our efforts to do good by private means. He shows both the opportunities offered by our great wealth, and the temptations to disingenuousness (accentuated recently, for example, by our tax laws). He shows how the dogmas of individualism and of equal opportunity, and the chance to rise in the world, have made the spirit of philanthropy sometimes seem at odds with the spirit of democracy.

Mr. Bremner does not deny that Americans, like other men, have often wanted simply to help their fellow men. But he shows how the facts of our history—our colonial origins, the American Revolution, the institution of slavery and the efforts to abolish it, the rise of an American Standard of Living, and the accumulation of industrial wealth—have provided temptations to misuse philanthropic slogans for personal, political, or economic ends, just as they have provided opportunities for the unalloyed philanthropic spirit.

By putting a familiar, but largely unexamined, American institution into the main stream of our civilization, Mr. Bremner admirably serves the purposes of the "Chicago History of American Civilization," which aims to make each aspect of our culture a window to all our history. The series contains two kinds of books: a *chronological* group, which provides a coherent narrative of American history from its beginning to the present day, and a *topical* group, which deals with the history of varied and significant aspects of American life. This

Editor's Preface

book is one of the topical group. Titles already published in the series are listed at the end of this book.

DANIEL J. BOORSTIN

Table of Contents

Introduction / 1

I.   Doing Good in the New World / 5

II. Religious and Revolutionary Humanitarianism / 20

III. Benevolence in the Young Republic / 42

IV. Saints and Scolds / 58

V.   Civil War Philanthropies / 76

VI. "Scientific Philanthropy" / 89

VII. Benevolent Trusts and Distrusts / 105

VIII. The Business of Benevolence and the Industry
of Destruction / 122

IX. A Time to Remember / 143

X.   A Voyage Is Now Proposed / 165

Important Dates / 187

Suggested Reading / 198

Acknowledgments / 213

Index / 215

Illustrations

Facing page

The Pennsylvania Hospital in 1800   38

Stephen Girard   39

Amos Lawrence   60

"Please Sir, May I Have a Bed." Newsboys' Lodging House of
    Children's Aid Society of New York, 1854   61

Clara Barton   108

Dorothea Dix   108

Andrew Carnegie   109

Advertisement of the President's Organization on Unemploy-
    ment Relief   158

Scene in ARC Roosevelt Club, Manila, 1946   159

Introduction

It's a serious, stern, responsible deed,
To help an unfortunate soul in his need.
And your one reward, when you quiet his plaint,
Is to feel like an opulent, careworn saint.

CLARENCE DAY

Ever since the seventeenth century, when Cotton Mather announced that Boston's helpfulness and readiness to every good work were well and favorably known in Heaven, Americans have regarded themselves as an unusually philanthropic people. In the twentieth century, celebration of American philanthropy has reached such heights that one can scarcely read a newspaper or magazine without being reminded, in editorials or advertisements, that the United States is the country with a heart, that giving is the great American game, and that philanthropy ranks as one of the leading industries of the age. Americans seem never to tire of saying, or of hearing, that they are generous to a fault—the most compassionate, open-handed people the world has ever known. The philanthropic streak in the national character is taken so much for granted that it is sometimes deemed more a genial failing than an asset or virtue.

As this tendency suggests, the word philanthropy and the ideas it carries with it arouse mixed emotions in American breasts. Many Americans have been concerned lest their countrymen's generosity be abused. But on a deeper level there is something about philanthropy that seems to go against the democratic grain. We may be willing to help others, but we are not humble enough to appreciate the efforts of those who would bend down to help us. "Don't try to uplift me," we say. "I can lift myself." We expect rich men to be generous with their wealth, and criticize them when they are not; but when they make benefaction, we question their motives, deplore the methods by which they obtained their abundance, and wonder whether their gifts will not do more harm than good.

Criticism of philanthropy and distrust of philanthropists are of course not peculiar to the United States, but there has been no lack of either in this country. Our literature abounds in portraits of foolish or hypocritical philanthropists. Newspaper and magazine editors decry the activities of "do gooders" and "bleeding hearts"; conservatives denounce "sentimental humanitarianism"; and radicals sneer at the "palliatives" offered by "mere philanthropic reform." The prejudice against philanthropy is felt even by its practitioners. Many of our most active and generous benefactors resent being called philanthropists and deny that their works have a philanthropic purpose. Until quite recently theoretical writings on the subject of philanthropy seem to have consisted mainly, and sometimes exclusively, in condemnations of "unwise giving."

Whether we approve or disapprove of philanthropy, the fact remains that it has been one of the principal methods of social advance. And we do not need to exaggerate the extent of our

Introduction

generosity to recognize that voluntary benevolence has played a large role and performed important functions in American society. Here, as elsewhere, philanthropy has covered a wider field than charity; the problems of the poor have not been philanthropy's only or even primary concern. The aim of philanthropy in its broadest sense is improvement in the quality of human life. Whatever motives animate individual philanthropists, the purpose of philanthropy itself is to promote the welfare, happiness, and culture of mankind.

We are all indebted to philanthropic reformers who have called attention to and agitated for abatement of the barbarities inflicted by society on its weaker members. We are all, in some degree, beneficiaries of philanthropy whenever we attend church, go to college, visit museums or concert halls, draw books from libraries, obtain treatment at hospitals, or spend leisure hours in parks. Most of us use, or may have occasion to use, institutions and services now tax-supported, which originated as philanthropic enterprises. We continue to rely on philanthropy for the support of scientific research, for experimentation in the field of social relations, and for diffusion of knowledge in all branches of learning.

The record of American philanthropy is so impressive that it would require several lengthy volumes to list its achievements. In a book as brief as this one, some of those achievements can only be alluded to, and many important benefactors and benefactions must be omitted. The author extends his apologies to readers who may look in vain in the following pages for mention of favorite philanthropists; many of the author's favorites have been left out too. The book is not an encyclopedia of good works but a narrative of some of the major trends in American philanthropy, broadly defined, set against the background of the main developments in American social history. The study is a survey of voluntary activity in the fields of charity, religion, education, humanitarian reform, social service, war relief, and foreign aid. It deals with representative donors, whether of money or service, with promoters of moral and social reform, and with the various institutions and associations Americans have founded to conduct their philanthropic business. The author hopes that the book will advance the growing interest in philanthropy as a subject of research and that the story told in the following pages will offer occasional insights into the character of American civilization.

I

Doing Good in the New World

If any man ask, Why it is so necessary to do good?
I must say, it sounds not like the question of a good
man.

COTTON MATHER

The earliest American philanthropists, as far as European
records go, were those gentle Indians of the Bahama Islands
who greeted Columbus at his first landfall in the New World.
In view of the cruelty and exploitation these natives were to
suffer at the hands of white men there is something ominous in
Columbus' report that they were "ingenuous and free" with all
they had, gave away anything that was asked of them, and
bestowed each gift "with as much love as if their hearts went
with it."

From other Indians pioneer white settlers obtained a wealth
of practical assistance in the difficult task of adjusting to life in
an alien land. The names of most of these benefactors are forgotten, but one at least is familiar to every schoolboy. Squanto,

who had once been kidnapped by an Englishman and carried off to be sold into slavery, escaped from bondage and returned to New England. There, during the starving time at Plymouth in the winter of 1620–21, Squanto proved "a special instrument sent of God" for the good of the enfeebled, bewildered Pilgrims. He taught them, in the words of William Bradford, "how to set their corn, where to take fish, and to procure other commodities, and was also their pilot to bring them to unknown places for their profit, and never left them till he died." Sad to relate, Squanto used his connections with the Pilgrims to extort gifts for himself from other Indians, and so his hands, like those of some other eminent philanthropists, were not entirely clean. On his deathbed he asked the governor "to pray for him that he might go to the Englishman's God in Heaven, and bequeathed sundry of his things to sundry of his English friends as remembrances of his love. . . ."

Philanthropy is philanthropy wherever and by whomever practiced. When we speak of American philanthropy, however, we usually have in mind an imported product rather than an indigenous growth. Our systems and principles of benevolence, both public and private, originated in Europe before the colonization of America began. They were brought to this country by Europeans, and their subsequent development was influenced by European experience and theory. For many years our philanthropic institutions sought and received support from abroad; and until quite recently those institutions were copies of European models. All we can lay claim to on the score of uniqueness is that philanthropy *in* America took such firm root and grew so prodigiously that it early assumed a stature and significance all its own.

To understand why this happened we must remember, first,

that the age of colonization coincided with one of the great periods of European philanthropy. The seventeenth century saw the launching of heroic missionary enterprises, a revival of interest in charitable works, the development in England of a system of tax-supported poor relief, and the organization of a host of associations for specialized philanthropic purposes. America inspired some of these undertakings and benefited directly or indirectly from nearly all of them, for the discovery of the New World affected the conscience as well as the cupidity of the Old. Almost every effort at colonization had, or claimed to have, a philanthropic motivation: there were natives to be converted to Christianity, poor men to be provided with land and work, and a wilderness to be supplied with the institutions of civilization. It is not too much to say that many Europeans regarded the American continent mainly as a vastly expanded field for the exercise of benevolence.

The real founders of American philanthropy, however, were men and women who crossed the Atlantic to establish communities that would be *better* than, instead of like or different from, the ones they had known at home. The Puritan leader, John Winthrop (1588–1649) forthrightly stated their purpose in the lay sermon, "A Model of Christian Charity," which he preached on the ship "Arbella" to "the great company of religious people" voyaging from old to New England in the year 1630. Winthrop used "Charity" as a synonym for love rather than in the modern sense of aid to the poor; and the "Model" he proposed was not a new scheme of benevolence but a code of conduct for a company of Christians who had entered into a covenant with God. The Puritans' God permitted no breach of contract but demanded strict performance of each article in the covenant. Therefore, as Winthrop said, "in this duty of love we must love brotherly without dissimulation, we must love one another with a pure heart fervently, we must bear one another's burdens, we must not look only on our own things but also on the things of our brethren. Neither must we think that the Lord will bear with such failings at our hands as He doth from those among whom we have lived. . . ."

Like later philanthropists, Winthrop justified disparities in wealth and condition as divinely ordained. He had no wish to tamper with God's design, and he did not hesitate to distinguish between "the great ones," "high and eminent in power and dignity," and "the poor and inferior sort" of men. Winthrop looked upon such distinctions as necessary for the good and preservation of society. He was convinced however, that no man was made richer or more honorable than his neighbor for his own sake, but only "for the glory of his creator and the common good of the creature man." The poor must not rise up against their superiors; neither should the rich and mighty be allowed to eat up the poor. Differences in condition existed, not to separate and alienate men from one another, but to make them have more need of each other, and to bind them closer together "in the bond of brotherly affection." And those differences, important and essential though Winthrop believed them to be, seemed less significant to him than "our community as members of the same body." "We must be knit together in this work as one man," he said. "We must delight in each other, make others' conditions our own, rejoice together, mourn together, labor and suffer together. . . ." The common objective—"to improve our lives to do more service to the Lord"—must never be lost sight of, and "the care of the public" must take precedence over all private interests.

Doing Good in the New World

Winthrop's vision of a community united and exalted by religious dedication was not to be realized even in Puritan New England. The mean and despised were not content to remain in the state to which God had assigned them; the powerful showed little disposition to forego opportunities to profit at the expense of the weak; and neither rich nor poor was willing to remain for long under the rule of divinely commissioned magistrates. Competition, individualism, and self-interest proved too strong to be suppressed, and what Roger Williams, in a letter to Winthrop's son, called "the common trinity of the world— Profit, Preferment, Pleasure"—soon made their appearance. Even so, Winthrop's ideal was never entirely forsaken. The forces of disunity, although they could not be held down, did not quite prevail; and, not only in the colonial period, but in later eras as well, Americans continued to feel under a special obligation to bring the duty of neighborly and brotherly love, everywhere professed, into "familiar and constant practice."

Half a century after Winthrop and the Puritans started to build their city upon a hill in New England, William Penn (1644–1718) began his holy experiment in Pennsylvania. Although Penn founded the colony as a refuge for Quakers and members of other persecuted sects, the idea of withdrawing from or renouncing the world had no place in his plans. "True Godliness," he said, "don't turn men out of the World, but enables them to live better in it, and excites their Endeavors to Mend it." To Penn and the Quakers there was no conflict between efforts to live better in the world and endeavors to improve it. The two were inseparably bound together, and the one was the means of achieving the other. Living better in the world meant following the rule of moderation or, more specifically, observing diligence (the middle path between drudgery and idleness) and frugality (as opposed to the extremes of miserliness and extravagance) in one's daily affairs. Mending the world was to be accomplished by employing the rewards of diligence and frugality for benevolent and humanitarian purposes—not casually and incidentally, but wholeheartedly—as the major business of life.

A good deal of the hostility the Quakers encountered arose from the fact that they regarded the conduct of daily life as much, if not more, a part of religious observance than formal worship. But the Quaker outlook, radical in its belief in separation of church and state and in its insistence upon the individual's right of freedom of conscience, was conservative in its attitude toward social organization. Penn, no less than Winthrop, deemed class distinctions an essential part of the divine order. God has not placed men "on the level," he said, but has arranged them in descending orders of subordination and dependency; due respect for these God-ordained differences required "Obedience to Superiors, Love to Equals, . . . *Help* and *Countenance* to Inferiors."

Assumptions of social superiority and inferiority, however, were typical of seventeenth-century thought rather than peculiar to the Quakers. Penn himself emphasized the responsibilities rather than the privileges that went with rank. He took the doctrine of stewardship both seriously and literally, believing that men were indebted to God not only for their wealth but for their very being, and accountable to Him for the way they spent their lives as well as their fortunes. His concept of stewardship was free of the condescension with which it is so often associated because, in his case, the doctrine of stewardship was joined to an equally serious and literal belief in the brotherhood of man. Penn was, after all, one of "The People called Friends," and, like other Quakers, he rejected the Calvinistic notion of the Elect. Whatever the differences in material conditions among men, all men were children of God, carriers of His seed, and spiritually equal in His sight.

Penn anticipated Benjamin Franklin in admiration for industry, thrift, and the other economic virtues that are now attributed to the middle class. Practical man that he was, Penn certainly had an appreciation for the value of money, but he believed that God gave men wealth to use rather than to love or hoard. Of all the vices, avarice struck him as worst. The spectacle of men, already comfortably fixed, who scrambled by day and plotted by night to increase their wealth moved him to scorn. "They are running up and down," he commented, "as if it were to save the life of a condemned innocent." Their conduct, personally disgraceful, was socially ruinous; for the reason the poor had too little was that the rich, already possessing too much, were striving to pile up even more.

Next to avarice Penn abhorred waste, display, and the pursuit of pleasure. Here again Penn's puritanical attitude expressed his social conscience: if all the money wasted on luxury and extravagance were put to public use, the wants of the poor would be well satisfied. To be sure, mortal man required diversion; but (or so Penn said), "The best recreation is to do good." There will be time enough for making merry "when the pale faces are more commiserated, the pinched bellies relieved and naked backs clothed, when the famished poor, the distressed widow, and the helpless orphan . . . are provided for."

Penn's writings, personal influence, and deeds left an indelible influence on Quakerdom and, through his followers, on nearly all subsequent humanitarian movements. Penn was, however, an Englishman. He visited America only twice, at widely separated intervals, and his total stay in this country amounted to no longer than four years. It is not Penn, therefore, but a native Yankee, the grandson of two of the founders of Massachusetts, who must be considered the chief exponent of do-goodism in colonial America.

Cotton Mather (1663–1728), unfortunately better remembered today for his part in the witchcraft trials than for his benevolent activities, is one of the commanding figures in the history of American philanthropy. The son of a president of Harvard, and himself one of the founders of Yale, Mather was the most prolific and conspicuously learned writer of the colonial period. Of the approximately four hundred and fifty works he is known to have published, one of the least pretentious, *Bonifacius*, or, as it is usually known, *Essays To Do Good* (1710), enjoyed the greatest and longest popularity. In it Mather proposed that men and women, acting either as individuals or as members of voluntary associations, should engage in "a perpetual endeavor to do good in the world." Such advice, coming from a son of the Puritans, was hardly novel. It was the method Mather outlined rather than the objective that was new. And it was this individualistic, voluntary method —taken not from the Quakers, whom Mather disliked, but from the German Pietists, especially August Hermann Francke of Halle—that was destined to characterize American philanthropy for many years to come.

In the passage quoted at the head of this chapter, Mather disposed in summary fashion of one of the persistent objections to the gospel and practice of doing good. It is interesting, however, to consider why Mather himself thought it so necessary to do good. He regarded the performance of good works as an obligation owed to God rather than as a means of salvation; yet, as a constant expounder of the doctrine of stewardship, he had no doubt that God would punish the unfaithful steward. Moreover, as he was frank enough to admit and bold enough to proclaim, doing good was a reward in itself. To help the unfortunate was an honor, a privilege, "an incomparable pleasure." Not content to let the case rest here, Mather cited an entire catalogue of worldly advantages including long life and business success he thought would surely accrue to the benevolent. Besides, as Mather took pains to point out, doing good was sound policy, a mild but effective instrument of social control. Pious example, moral leadership, voluntary effort, and private charity were the means by which competing and conflicting interests in society might be brought into harmony.

To Mather charity emphatically did begin at home; for he believed that each man must start his career of doing good by correcting whatever was amiss in his own heart and life. Yet for all the emphasis on personal reform, Mather's was a social gospel. Keep a list of the needy in your neighborhood, he urged his readers; be on the lookout for persons who may require help, and seize each opportunity to be useful with "rapturous assiduity." Always bear in mind that "charity to the *souls* of men" is the highest form of benevolence. Send preachers, Bibles, and other books of piety to heathens at home and abroad; support the church, and keep a watchful eye on the spiritual health of the community. Very often, he said, the poor need "admonitions of piety" quite as much as alms. "Cannot you contrive to mingle a spiritual charity with your temporal bounty?"

Mather's own charitable gifts were sufficient to make him a one-man relief and aid society. But Mather's real contribution to the practice of philanthropy lay in his recognition of the need for enlisting the support of others in benevolent enterprises. He was a tireless promoter of associations for distributing tracts, supporting missions, relieving needy clergymen, and building churches in poor communities. At the same time, in sermons and private conversations, he called the attention of the rich to the needs, physical as well as spiritual, of the poor. From personal experience he learned that the recompense of the charitable was multiplication of occasions to be serviceable. "Those who devote themselves to good devices," he drily observed, "usually find a wonderful increase of their opportunities." In a beautiful simile he likened a good deed to "a stone falling into a pool—one circle and service will produce another, till they extend—who can tell how far?"

Despite, or as Mather would have said, because of his sincere concern for the poor, he advocated extreme care in the bestowal of alms. "Let us try to do good with as much application of mind as wicked men employ in doing evil," was his motto. Giving wisely was therefore an even greater obligation than giving generously; and withholding alms from the undeserving as needful and essentially benevolent as bestowing them on the deserving. In a famous and widely approved sermon delivered in 1698 Mather told the good people of Boston: "Instead of exhorting you to augment your charity, I will rather utter an exhortation . . . that you may not *abuse* your charity by misapplying it." He was disturbed by the increase of idleness and fearful that an excess of benevolence might nourish and confirm the idle in their evil ways. "The poor that can't work are objects for your liberality," he said. "But the poor that *can* work and *won't*, the best liberality to them is to *make* them." The thing to do was to cure them of their idleness: "Find 'em work; set 'em to work; keep 'em to work. Then, as much of your bounty to them as you please."

The most famous tribute to the *Essays To Do Good* came from an unlikely source. In youth—actually boyhood—Benjamin Franklin (1706–90) had been an enemy of the Mathers, and the pseudonym adopted in his earliest published work, Silence Dogood, was an unkind thrust at Cotton Mather. In old age, however, Franklin advised Samuel Mather, Cotton's son, that the *Essays* had influenced his conduct throughout life. "I have always set a greater value on the character of a *doer of good*, than on any other kind of reputation," he wrote, "and if I have been . . . a useful citizen, the public owes the advantage of it to that book."

Franklin did not acknowledge and possibly was not aware of the influence Quakerism exerted on his character and career. Nevertheless there was much in his approach to life that bore witness to his prolonged association with the Friends. He did not learn the virtues of discretion, moderation, and attention to his business from his first master, his brother James; in these, as in so many other arts, Franklin was self-taught. Yet he presumably derived something, if only concern for reputability, from the example of solid Quaker businessmen for whom he worked as a young man and whose patronage he solicited when he entered business for himself. At any rate it was a happy circumstance that Franklin, with his Puritan background and avowed indebtedness to Mather, should have carried out his highly successful experiments in useful living in the city founded by William Penn.

In addition to numerous similarities, there was a significant difference between Franklin's views and those of Penn and Mather. Penn demanded that money, instead of being hoarded or spent on impious luxuries, should be used for comforting the poor. Mather dreamed of a city in which each house would have an alms-box bearing the message *"Think* on the Poor." Franklin, however, conceived of a society in which there would be no poor and little need for relief or charity. He sprang from a different class and addressed himself to a different audience than Penn or Mather. Far from forgetting his humble origin, he traded on it throughout life. In the successive volumes of *Poor Richard's Almanack* Franklin spoke to "leather-aproned" folk as a man of their own sort. As he preached it, the gospel of industry, frugality, and sobriety was worldly wisdom rather than spiritual discipline. Contrary to what is sometimes assumed, Franklin did not advise his readers to seek riches or tell them how to gain wealth. If he had really wanted to do so, with his knowledge of the world, he could have offered more practical suggestions than maxims of self-help. It was the road to independence, not the "Way to Wealth" that Franklin pointed out. "Be *industrious* and *free;* be *frugal* and *free,*" he counseled—free among other things of dependency upon the uncertain charity of the world.

In conducting his own affairs Franklin observed the maxims of the *Almanack,* if not to the letter, closely enough to become financially independent at a relatively early age. At forty-two he sold his printing house and devoted most of the rest of his life to serving the public. Long before quitting business, however, he had begun to practice what he so often preached to others: "Leisure is Time for doing something useful." It goes without saying that Franklin used his leisure to advance his own knowledge and reputation; but he employed it as earnestly for social as for self-improvement. Although the fact is well known, it is worth recalling that instead of patenting and seeking profit from his inventions, Franklin willingly gave the products of his ingenuity to the world. He introduced a secular spirit into the do-good gospel and shifted the emphasis from pious works and personal charity to efforts to further the general welfare. To Franklin, God was "the Great Benefactor." His religion consisted in the belief that men should show their gratitude to God "by the only means in their power, promoting the happiness of his other children."

Franklin was above all a man of the eighteenth century and it is not wise to insist too strongly on the modernity of his approach to social problems. In much that he did or suggested, however, it is possible to recognize principles that later came to be recognized as characteristic both of enlightened public policy and of constructive philanthropy. Preventing poverty always impressed him as a more sensible course than relieving it. In calling for repeal of the poor laws on the ground that public provision for the needy had an even greater tendency than almsgiving to pauperize the poor, Franklin went beyond Mather, who had warned of the abuses of private charity, and foreshadowed the scientific philanthropists and reformers of the nineteenth century. "I am for doing good to the poor," he wrote "but I differ in opinion about the means. I think the best way of doing good to the poor is, not making them easy *in* poverty, but leading or driving them out of it." In practice Franklin relied on leading rather than driving, on persuasion and encouragement rather than coercion. Unlike some later advocates of individualism, however, Franklin was not content merely to exhort the poor to become self-supporting. He was ever mindful of the need for widening opportunities for self-help, and throughout life he strove, as he put it, "to promote the happiness of mankind" by working for the establishment of conditions in which men would be able to take care of themselves.

Franklin's philanthropic activities, although varied, followed a consistent pattern. Starting in 1727 with the Junto, a club for the mutual improvement of its members, and the library (1731) which was the Junto's first offshoot, Franklin proceeded to organize or assist in organizing a host of civic projects. He founded a volunteer fire company, developed schemes for paving, cleaning, and lighting the streets of Philadelphia, and sponsored a plan for policing the city. His political talents were never better displayed than in his ability to unite public and private support behind municipal improvements. He played a leading part in the establishment of both the Pennsylvania Hospital (1751) and the academy which became the University of Pennsylvania. Funds provided in his will made possible the founding, more than a century after his death, of a technical institute in Boston. His interest in "improving the common Stock of Knowledge" led to the formation in 1743 of the American Philosophical Society, the first and for many years the foremost American institution for promoting research in the natural and social sciences.

Franklin demonstrated that the sovereign remedy of self-help, so often prescribed for individuals, could be applied with equally beneficial results to society. He did not invent the principle of improving social conditions through voluntary associations, but more than any American before him he showed the availability, usefulness, and appropriateness of that method to American conditions. The voluntary method, as Franklin's success with it suggested, and as later events were to prove, was precisely suited to the inclinations of his countrymen.

II

Religious and Revolutionary Humanitarianism

The Humane Mania: . . . Persons afflicted with this madness, feel for every species of distress, and seem to pour forth tears upon some occasions, from every pore of their bodies. . . . Gracious heaven! if ever I should be visited with this species of madness, . . . my constant prayer to the divine fountain of justice and pity—shall be, that *I may never be cured of it.*

BENJAMIN RUSH

In the third and fourth decades of the eighteenth century a series of religious revivals collectively known as the Great Awakening, swept over the American colonies. The revival fervor reached its peak around 1742 and thereafter quickly subsided, perishing, as Jonathan Edwards' biographer has written, in its own noise. Brief though its sway, the Great Awakening effected what may with some slight exaggeration be called an American Reformation, for by strengthening in-

Religious and Revolutionary Humanitarianism

dividual religiosity it encouraged a spirit of religious independence and thus weakened the authority of the churches. George Whitefield (1714–70), Jonathan Edwards (1703–58), and other preachers of the revival made religion an intensely personal concern. Their emphasis on an inner experience of spiritual rebirth revealed possibilities of a whole religious existence outside the established forms of worship. The number of churches, sects, and church members increased as a result of the Awakening, but never again would the hold of the meeting house on individual consciences be secure, and never again would organized religion provide the only outlet for men's strivings for a better life. While religious and sectarian charities continued to flourish, a vast new interest in secular and humanitarian philanthropies developed both within and without the churches.

Among the most important results of the Great Awakening were the fostering of humane attitudes and the popularization of philanthropy at all levels of society, but especially among the poorer classes. The Awakening was a mass movement. It derived its strength from, and made its greatest impact on, humble men and women, many of whom belonged to no church and were therefore beyond the reach of religious appeals for charity. The revival gave them an opportunity to indulge in sentiments usually regarded as above their proper station in life and to partake more fully in the pleasures of piety and benevolence. Of all the conversions wrought by the Great Awakening certainly the most remarkable was the transformation of do-goodism from a predominantly upper- and middle-class activity—half responsibility, half recreation—into a broadly shared, genuinely popular avocation.

The man chiefly responsible for this achievement was George

American Philanthropy

Whitefield a young English evangelist who had not yet turned twenty-five when, in the autumn of 1739, he began the most famous preaching tour in American history. On this, the second of the seven visits Whitefield was to make to the colonies, he spent fourteen months (in his own words) "ranging and hunting the American woods after poor sinners." Whitefield found the quarry eager to be caught, for the fame of his eloquence had preceded him across the Atlantic and earlier revivals in the middle colonies and New England had prepared the way for his message of the awful need and wondrous possibilities of a new birth in Christ. The Awakening was already in progress when Whitefield arrived. He linked isolated, local revivals into an intercolonial movement, and turned the torrents of religious excitement unloosed by these revivals in the direction of practical benevolence.

It was not only the suffering of the damned but the misery of the poor that Whitefield preached. Other exhorters equaled or excelled him in ability to terrorize audiences with threats of hell-fire, but none approached him in ability to move the hearts and purses of listeners. He appealed to conscience and altruism as well as to fear, pleaded as earnestly for money as for souls, and made the collection plate hardly less important than the mourners' bench. With his superb voice, extraordinary histrionic talent, and instinctive feeling for human interests he could stir vast throngs to frenzies of pity and remorse. Responding generously, even extravagantly, to Whitefield's cry for alms became more than a demonstration of piety: it was a welcome and almost essential means of relieving emotional tension.

The principal object of the donations Whitefield collected was an orphanage, modeled after Francke's celebrated institution in Halle, which he founded in the impoverished colony of Georgia in 1740. This project, although appealing, was not well thought out and proved to be a costly undertaking. Whitefield raised money for the orphanage in England as well as in America; he purchased and operated a slave-manned plantation in South Carolina to obtain additional revenue for its support; and agitated for removal of the prohibition of slavery in the Georgia charter. For thirty years Whitefield devoted as much care to the management of the institution as the circumstances of his career permitted. In the closing years of his life he tried vainly to turn the orphanage into a college. Whitefield, however, was a better fund-raiser than administrator; and despite the energy and expense he lavished on the orphan home it never fulfilled his expectations.

The indifferent success of Whitefield's pet charity did not dampen his enthusiasm for benevolence. Throughout his mature life he made it his practice to improve his acquaintance with the rich for the benefit of the poor. Like Cotton Mather, whom Whitefield resembled in this respect, if in no other, he was ever ready to find support for good causes. He took up collections for poor debtors, raised money for victims of disaster, and secured books and financial assistance for hard-pressed colonial colleges. Harvard, Dartmouth, Princeton, and the University of Pennsylvania all benefited from his assistance. If no single institution can be regarded as his monument, the reason is partly that he helped so many.

The thirty-odd years between the Great Awakening and the Revolution brought a succession of emergencies that placed severe strains on American philanthropy. During much of the period the colonies were officially, if not always actively, at war with the French and Indians. The problem of poor relief, serious even before 1740, was made still more acute by the military struggle. Disabled soldiers, displaced Acadians, and refugees from the frontier swelled the numbers of the orphaned, widowed, aged, ill, and improvident for whom care had to be provided. The ranks of the distressed were further increased by two serious depressions, an influx of needy immigrants, recurring epidemics of smallpox, dysentery, and other diseases, and destructive fires in Charleston, South Carolina, and Boston. Despite the humanitarian sentiments spread by the Awakening, colonial society was poorly equipped to deal with these accumulated misfortunes. Private fortunes were too few and wealth neither widely enough distributed nor sufficiently fluid to permit large-scale or sustained private giving. Public relief under the poor laws was ordinarily available only to persons having legal settlement in a given community. In Massachusetts and some other colonies provincial legislatures reimbursed towns for the care of refugees and certain other needy wanderers who could not meet residence requirements for local relief. In time of depression or disaster, however, communities were hard put to care for their own poor.

In these circumstances welfare necessarily became a joint public-private partnership. Services that could not otherwise have been provided could be, and were, established through the willingness of public bodies and private citizens each to assist and supplement the philanthropic activities of the other. This co-operative approach was an expedient, but in view of the antagonism later thought to exist between governmental and voluntary efforts in the field of welfare, it stands out as one of the noteworthy aspects of colonial philanthropy. The line between public and private responsibility was not sharply drawn. In seasons of distress overseers of the poor frequently called on the churches for special collections of alms, and throughout the colonial period giving or bequeathing property to public authorities for charitable purposes remained a favorite form of philanthropy. Friendly societies organized along national, occupational, or religious lines relieved public officials of the necessity for caring for some of the poor by supplying mutual aid to members and dispensing charity to certain categories of beneficiaries. New institutions, notably the Pennsylvania Hospital and the Philadelphia Bettering House, jointly financed by taxation and private contributions, offered unsurpassed facilities for treating and sheltering the poor. Gifts from overseas, added to funds raised by colonial churches and assemblies, made possible the founding of new colleges, better support for those already in existence, and an expansion of missionary and educational work among the Indians.

The sponsors of these undertakings appealed to common sense and self-interest as well as to compassion. Certainly this was true of the friendly societies, which, in addition to performing charitable and convivial services, gave members a sense of economic security. Dr. Thomas Bond (1712–84), the principal founder of the Pennsylvania Hospital, presented the project as "a means of increasing the Number of People, and preserving many useful Members to the Public from Ruin and Distress." The Philadelphia Bettering House and similar houses of industry in other cities asked and received support on the grounds that they not only relieved but employed the destitute, promoted industry and frugality among the poor, and thereby reduced the number of beggars and paupers. Eleazar Wheelock's (1711–79) success in obtaining money for his Indian school (later Dartmouth College) stemmed partly from his argument that the spread of Christianity and civilization among the tribesmen would provide "a far better Defense than all our expensive Fortresses."

Such rationalizations, although useful in giving humane motives a practical justification, are not sufficient to explain the vigor of colonial philanthropy. More revealing than these public pronouncements is the private observation of John Smith, a Philadelphia Quaker, who wrote in his diary in 1747 that he had not yet turned any beggar away empty handed, since "a fellow feeling of the Infirmities and wants of our Brethren—as all mankind are—is a duty, and not sufficiently practiced without Administering Relief when in our power." How seriously Americans took that duty became clear in 1760 when individuals, churches, town meetings, and legislatures throughout the colonies raised impressive sums for the relief of Boston's fire sufferers. Fourteen years later the closing of Boston's harbor in punishment for the Boston Tea Party threatened that city with economic ruin and produced the greatest relief crisis in the colonial period. Once again, but even more generously than before, other towns and colonies dispatched money, clothing, food, and livestock to Boston as if to prove that Americans, although not yet united politically, were already knit together by bonds of sympathy and affection.

Anthony Benezet (1713–84) was one of the men who drafted an appeal to Pennsylvania and New Jersey Quakers asking contributions for the relief of "the necessitous of every religious denomination" in Boston and other afflicted areas of New England. It was not the first time that the French-born Benezet, always frail in health and almost as poor as those he helped, had lent his assistance to such tasks. At the start of the French and Indian War he had organized relief for frontier settlers driven from their homes by Indian raids; and for more than a decade after 1756 he had been the self-appointed guardian of the Acadians in Philadelphia, obtaining grants for these French-Catholic war victims from a grudging legislature and begging gifts for them from his fellow Quakers. Benezet had come to Pennsylvania in 1731 and was by profession a schoolmaster. By 1775 he had instructed a fair portion of the youth of Philadelphia—rich and poor, boys and girls, black and white. Meanwhile, through unflagging efforts as almoner and pamphleteer, he had extended his pedagogy to the entire community. Justice, and charity in the old sense of love, were the lessons Benezet taught. Because his conscience was alert to wrong as well as misfortune, and because he not only labored to ameliorate suffering, but courageously exposed and fought injustice, he deserves to rank as one of America's first humanitarian reformers.

The most famous picture of Benezet is Benjamin Rush's recollection of him as he appeared in old age: "His face was grave, placid, and full of benignity. In one hand he carried a subscription paper and a petition; in the other he carried a small pamphlet on the unlawfulness of the African Slave-trade, and a letter directed to the King of Prussia, upon the unlawfulness of war." "He is small, old and ugly," said a French officer during the American Revolution, "but his countenance wears the stamp of a peaceful soul and the repose of a good conscience." That benign countenance masked a ready wit and sharp tongue. Benezet laughed tolerantly when he heard that an aged Acadian, long a beneficiary of his charity, had concluded that such kindness as Benezet had shown over so many years could not possibly be disinterested, and that the author of it must have some design to profit at the expense of the

Acadians. For the ungenerous, however, especially those of his own sect, Benezet had nothing but scorn. He told his friend John Smith that he was weary of begging vainly of men who could afford to give a thousand pounds "without having one tear the less dropt on that account by their Heirs." It was no excuse for these men to say that they were insufficiently acquainted with the misery of the poor: they did not wait for full details before acting when they heard rumors that some extraordinary bargain might easily be attained. "The appellation of *Steward* is what we often take upon ourselves," he observed, "but indeed, in the mouth of many it is but a cant, unmeaning expression."

Benezet accompanied his services to war sufferers with an attack on war itself. Men of letters have exposed the follies of prejudice and intolerance, he observed in 1780; "Will they not endeavor too, to disgust men with the horrors of war, and to make them live together like friends and brethren?" Benezet, at least, was willing to make the endeavor and he pressed the campaign most strenuously when it was least politic to do so, that is, in the midst of war. He wrote the letter to Frederick the Great, to which Rush alluded, in 1776. Inclosed with the letter was his pamphlet, "Thoughts on the Nature of War," first printed in 1766 and reissued in the year of Independence. Benezet also sent the pamphlet to Henry Laurens, president of the Continental Congress. Two years later he prepared another antiwar tract and presented copies to members of Congress, governors of states, and influential persons on both sides of the Atlantic. "If people had never seen War kindled in countries and between neighboring Nations, they could hardly believe that man would be so inattentive to the dictates of Reason, the tender feelings of humanity, and the Gospel . . . as deliberately to engage in battles for the destruction of each other," he told his readers. We should pray, he said, "not for the destruction of our enemies, who are still our Brethren, . . . ; but for an agreement with them."

Benezet devoted much of his voluminous correspondence and some of his most trenchant pamphlets to improving relations between Indians and whites. He was not alone in this work, but unlike some of his contemporaries, who were interested mainly in baptizing the Indians and making them allies in war and trade, Benezet's concern was to obtain consideration for Indians as fellow beings, and to secure recognition for them of rights to which they—in his opinion—were as much entitled as any other people. He publicized every instance that came to his attention of the friendly disposition of Indian chiefs or tribesmen. "Is it not notorious that they are generally kinder to us than we are to them?" he asked in the last of his many pamphlets. The difference between us and them, he said, "is chiefly owing to our different ways of life, and different ideas of what is necessary and desirable." The advantage we have over them is one of education "which puts it in our power to gloss over our own conduct, however evil; and to see theirs, however defensible, in the most odious point of light."

Of all the crusades in which Benezet engaged, the most fruitful was his long struggle in behalf of the Negro. Benezet, in common with his friend John Woolman (1720–72), was troubled by the effect of slaveholding on the religion and morals of slaveowners; and, like Woolman, he was particularly distressed at the countenancing of slavery by his own sect. In 1776, after more than twenty years of effort, he succeeded in bringing Philadelphia Friends to agree to censure and disown members of the Society who refused to give up their slaves. But Benezet was animated more by love for the Negro as a brother creature than by hatred for slaveholders. In his first important defense of Negro rights, written in 1754, he argued that if we sincerely desire to live by the golden rule, "we shall never think of bereaving our fellow-creatures of that valuable blessing liberty, nor endure to grow rich by their bondage." "Let us make their case our own," he continued, "and consider what we should think, and how we should feel, were we in their circumstances."

Through experience gained as a teacher of both Negro and white children Benezet had come to believe that there was as great a variety of talent in the one race as in the other and that the notion of Negro inferiority in intellectual capacity was "a vulgar prejudice." Combatting racial prejudice and showing that white superiority was based on illegal force and unjust laws became his major mission in life. In pamphlet after pamphlet he returned to the theme of Negro equality. Thus, on the eve of the Revolution— "at a time," as Benezet said, "when the general rights and liberties of mankind" were ardently proclaimed—he raised the question that still haunts Americans: How can "those who distinguish themselves as the advocates of liberty" deny equality and justice to others on the grounds of race?

Benezet showered his letters and pamphlets on those he thought would benefit from them as liberally as a rich man might have scattered alms. Two thousand copies of *A Caution and Warning to Great Britain and Her Colonies* (1767) went to the Society of Friends in London for distribution to members of Parliament and officers of the crown. An expanded version of this attack on the slave trade appeared in 1771 under the title *Some Historical Account of Guinea*. This book, also widely distributed, made a strong impression on John Wesley, who borrowed from it in his own *Thoughts on Slavery* (1774). Thomas Clarkson, the chief English foe of the slave trade, called Benezet's work "influential, beyond any other book ever before published, in disseminating a proper knowledge and detestation of this trade."

During the 1770's Benezet enlisted the support of the young physician Benjamin Rush in the fight against the slave trade, and he encouraged the antislavery views of his old friend and neighbor, Benjamin Franklin. Benezet lived long enough to lobby for the passage of Pennsylvania's gradual emancipation act of 1780, the first abolition law passed by any American state. After Benezet's death in 1784 Rush and Franklin reconstituted an association Benezet had founded to assist free Negroes into the Pennsylvania Society for Promoting the Abolition of Slavery. Franklin's last public act was to forward a petition of the Abolition Society to the First Congress urging that body to go to the very limit of its powers to discourage the traffic in human beings; and his last publication, as witty as anything he ever wrote, was a parody of the proslavery arguments advanced against the petition.

Benjamin Rush (1746–1813) was a generation younger than Benezet and Franklin—which means that he belonged to that remarkable group of Americans, born around the time of the Great Awakening, who came to maturity, and in a sense were reborn, during the American Revolution. Rush was a physician, teacher, soldier, statesman, writer, and, in all his callings, a reformer. The breadth of his interests was matched only by the intensity of his feelings. He approached every issue not only as though his own life were at stake but as if the fate of the world hung in balance. As a boy of fifteen he found and stated his life-mission: "to spend and be spent for the Good of Mankind is what I chiefly aim at."

Rush's ancestors included Quakers, Episcopalians, and Baptists but he grew up in an atmosphere of revivalistic Presbyterianism. His pastor, whom he eulogized in his earliest known publication, was the great revivalist, Gilbert Tennent. He studied under an uncle, Samuel Finley, who was a leader of the "New Light" wing of Presbyterianism, and he received his B.A. at the Presbyterian stronghold of Princeton. Rush met Whitefield as a boy and renewed his acquaintance with him while studying medicine in London during the late 1760's. For the rest of his life Rush treasured "the original, pious and eloquent sayings" of Whitefield and felt that he had been particularly fortunate to have known him.

In later years Rush rejected the Calvinistic doctrines in which he had been trained, but he never shed his youthful religiosity. He had a puritanical attitude toward idleness, deplored the use of tobacco and distilled liquors on grounds of morals as well as health, advocated adoption of the Bible as a school-book, and was acutely disturbed by the sin of Sabbath-breaking. "The clergy and their faithful followers of every denomination are *too good to do good*" he complained on one occasion. "It is possible we may not live to witness the approaching regeneration of our world," he wrote a friend, "but the more active we are in bringing it about, the more fitted we shall be for that world where justice and benevolence eternally prevail." Rush was given to visions, which he called dreams, and in one of them he envisaged Philadelphia spared from justly deserved destruction on several occasions by the intervention of the Angel of Mercy who, in each emergency, was able to point out some philanthropy sufficient to appease God's wrath.

In choosing a career Rush wavered between the ministry and medicine. Although he chose medicine, we may wonder whether religion did not really win out in the end. At almost any time in his life he might have said what he actually did say in a letter written while a medical apprentice: "Though now I pursue the study of physic, I am far from giving it any pre-eminence to Divinity." The Bible passage which he took most to heart and quoted most often "The son of Man is not come to *destroy* men's lives but to *save* them"—gave religious justification to the practice of medicine. Rush was a great physician and quite naturally believed that the principles of what he called "the healing art" could be applied to society. But his medical opinions, far from affecting his religious views, were themselves influenced by religion. There was something theological in Rush's belief in the unity of disease, something evangelical in his teaching and preaching of the one sure cure for all ailments, and a family resemblance between the drastic remedies he employed in effecting cures and the violent methods used by the revival preachers to obtain conversions.

For Rush, as for others of his generation, the American Revolution was the central experience of life. "This great event has everywhere shaken the human mind to its centre" he wrote in 1788. A quarter of a century after Independence he said "I still believe the American Revolution to be big with important consequences to the world, and that the labor of no individual, however feeble his contributions to it were, could have been spared." Rush, not yet thirty when the war began, had already gained some notoriety as a reformer through his tracts on temperance and the slave trade. In 1775 he encouraged

33

another pamphleteer, Thomas Paine, to write an appeal for American independence. Rush read drafts of the work as Paine composed it and suggested *Common Sense* as the title. He was a member of the Continental Congress, a signer of the Declaration of Independence, and, for about a year, surgeon-general and physician-general of Washington's army. In the latter posts Rush's zeal for improving medical services embroiled him in disputes with brother officers, and his criticism of superiors, including Washington, forced his resignation early in 1778.

The Revolution intensified the sense of mission that already possessed Rush. Termination of his military career, instead of disgusting him with the struggle, strengthened his ardor for the cause of liberty. Possibly because his participation in the war was so brief and unsatisfying, he continued to wage the Revolution on other fronts long after Independence had been won. The war is over, he was fond of saying, but the Revolution has just begun. The more important and the more difficult task of bringing "the principles, morals, and manners of our citizens" into harmony with republican institutions remained to be accomplished.

In the decade after 1783 Rush addressed himself to this task with energy and conviction seldom matched by any American reformer. "The world seems to be on the eve of a great change for the better," he exulted in 1787, and he rejoiced in the privilege of speeding the better day. In the midst of a growing medical practice he continued his political activities, took on new teaching duties, founded the Philadelphia Dispensary, the first free medical clinic in the United States, and began the study of mental disease and the experiments in humane treatment of the insane that were to be among his greatest services to the medical profession. Meanwhile he renewed his attack on slavery and strong drink; he wrote against tobacco and in favor of the sugar maple tree, cultivation of which he believed would free the world from dependence upon slave-produced West Indian cane sugar. He agitated for moderation of the criminal laws, opposed capital punishment and all public punishments, and sought to convert prisons into agencies of repentance and reform. A teacher himself, Rush tried to excite public interest in education in every form, at all levels, and for both sexes. He advocated establishment of free public schools, gave enthusiastic support to movements for broadening opportunities for higher education, and proposed reforms in school curriculum, teaching methods, and discipline. In one of his letters he referred to "a new pamphlet written by that turbulent spirit Dr. Rush, who I hope will never be quiet while there is ignorance, slavery, or misery in Pennsylvania." A correspondent, half-admiring, half-despairing of Rush's efforts likened him to Mr. Great Heart in *Pilgrim's Progress*.

Rush professed little respect for "the cold blood of common sense" but he frequently appealed to this sentiment in his pleas for reform. Noting the moderate expense involved in treating large numbers of needy patients at the Philadelphia Dispensary, he declared that the principles of mechanics had been applied to morals, "for in what other way would so great a weight of evil have been removed by so small a force?" He defined capital punishment as the punishment of murder by murder and called it an act of legal revenge which did no practical good and much demonstrable harm. In arguing for milder discipline in the classroom Rush pointed out that schoolmasters were the only despots still tolerated in free countries. He defended public expenditure for education as true economy, since, in his opinion, diffusion of education could result only in promoting order, prosperity, and morality and thus in lessening of taxes. We can never suppress vice and immorality by enacting laws against them, he asserted, but we can prevent them from becoming serious problems by making adequate provision for the instruction of the manners and morals of young people.

Varied though Rush's crusades were, and whimsical as some of his arguments seem, they were parts of a consistent and nobly conceived design. In the years of hope and promise that followed the Revolution, Rush directed his anger not at individuals but at the relics of barbarism in human institutions. The doctrines of universal salvation which he embraced in the 1780's bound him, as he said, to the whole human race. "I was animated constantly by a belief that I was acting for the benefit of the whole world, and for future ages," he recalled years later. He thought that Independence offered Americans a God-given opportunity, if not obligation, to root out old errors and vices and to erect a society whose humanity, civilization, and Christianity would be a beacon to the world. Rush was sanguine of the outcome for, as he wrote John Howard the English prison reformer in 1789, "we are at present in a *forming* state. We have as yet but few habits of any kind, and *good* ones may be acquired and fixed by a good example and proper instruction as easily as *bad* ones. . . ."

Ironically enough, it was a local emergency and the needs of Rush's own time which called forth his greatest efforts, brought him most fame, and involved him in the bitterest and longest controversies of his career. The emergency was an epidemic of yellow fever—the worst calamity of its kind in American history—which almost decimated the population of

Religious and Revolutionary Humanitarianism

Philadelphia between August and November of 1793. In the epidemic Rush lost his sister, three of his apprentices, many of his friends, and more of his patients than he liked to admit. He himself suffered three attacks of the fever, but as long as his strength permitted he treated all who asked for his help. During one week in September he estimated that he called on and prescribed for between 100 and 120 patients a day, while his apprentices visited from 20 to 25 more. For many weeks he carried on consultations even while taking his meals; and after his own illness confined him to his home, he reported, "In my parlor, on my couch, and even in my bed I prescribe for 50 to 100 people, chiefly the poor, every day."

It was characteristic of Rush that, in the very depth of disaster, he could say, "Never was the healing art so truly delightful to me." It was also characteristic of him to deal with the epidemic in the manner of a reformer. He maintained, in the first place, that the fever was generated locally by filth and that it could be prevented by improved sanitary practices. This view involved him in protracted disputes with those who deemed his opinion a slur on the good name of Philadelphia and who insisted that yellow fever was an imported pestilence to be stopped by stricter quarantine. Even sharper controversies arose, however, over Rush's remedy for the disease. He did not claim to have discovered, but he practiced and publicized what he called "the successful mode of treating" yellow fever. The treatment consisted of extremely strong purges followed by copious bloodletting. In private letters and public pronouncements Rush boasted of "the triumphs of mercury, jalap, and blood letting." He stoutly maintained that if administered early enough the remedy was a sure cure for yellow fever. Rush's remedy, which we now know was ineffective, was

37

The Pennsylvania Hospital in 1800. Engraving by William Birch. (From R. M. Palmer, *Reproduction of Birch's Celebrated Views of Philadelphia*, Philadelphia, 1908.)

widely condemned as well as devoutly praised in his own day. There can be no doubt, however, that Rush's faith in his cure and the confidence he inspired in others were factors in quieting the panic that accompanied the early stages of the epidemic.

While the doctors were disagreeing and the sick dying, with or without benefit of "the successful mode" of treatment, many residents of Philadelphia fled the city. Among those who stayed behind were the mayor, Matthew Clarkson, and a small group of public spirited citizens. These men organized themselves into a voluntary committee to carry on the normal business of the city and to provide the extraordinary services made necessary by the epidemic. To the best of their abilities and resources, and in a heriocally matter-of-fact spirit, they combatted the panic, tended the sick, buried the dead, and cared for the poor, the unemployed, the abandoned, and orphaned.

Perhaps the least likely candidate for heroism in this valiant band of volunteers was the squint-eyed, close-mouthed businessman, Stephen Girard. At the time of the epidemic Girard was forty-three years old, a self-made man whose gospel was work, laissez faire, and *caveat emptor*. Born in France, in 1750 (d. 1831), Girard had left home as a boy, and, after a dozen years of seafaring, had settled in Philadelphia at the start of the Revolution. For a decade or more before 1793 he had been engaged in trading ventures with the French West Indies. It was a lucrative business, but sometimes dubious and always risky. In the summer of 1793 Girard's affairs were more unsettled than usual owing to the slave uprising in Santo Domingo, and for a while he was more disturbed by disorders in the West Indies than by yellow fever in Philadelphia. "It seems as if the misfortunes at Cap Français will be fatal to me,"

Stephen Girard. (From E. A. Duyckinck, *National Portrait Gallery of Eminent Americans*, New York: Johnson, Fry & Co., 1862.)

he wrote to a business associate early in September, adding that the so-called plague in Philadelphia was "only a malignant fever which, by the pernicious treatment of our doctors, has sent many of our citizens to another world." He had easily thrown off a slight case of the fever, and he resented the interruption of business caused by the panic. "It is to be hoped," he wrote, "that the month of September will bring all the inhabitants back to their homes, and that business will resume its usual trend."

Before the month was half gone, however, Girard notified his correspondent that fear, fright, and disease had reduced the city to a deplorable condition. "I shall accordingly be very busy for a few days," he advised, "and if I have the misfortune to be overcome by the fatigues of my labor I shall have the satisfaction of having performed a duty which we owe to one another." The few days stretched into two months. The duty, voluntarily assumed, was the arduous and unpleasant one of administering the pesthouse established in an old mansion on Bush Hill. With the help of another volunteer, Peter Helm, and a French doctor, Jean Devèze (emphatically not a follower of Rush), Girard made the makeshift hospital into a model institution. The managers of Bush Hill could claim no miraculous cures. Most of their patients came to them in advanced stages of the disease, and about half of them died. But Girard's businesslike management, combined with the tender care he and his staff rendered to the sick and dying, turned Bush Hill from a place of horror into a haven of mercy.

Neither before nor after the epidemic were Rush and Girard on friendly terms. To Rush, Girard's character seemed as singular as his prosperity was extraordinary. He believed and repeated rumors of Girard's niggardliness toward impecunious relatives and of his despotic treatment of employees. "*Men will be Gods!*" he exclaimed in his commonplace book after recording instances of Girard's arrogance. For his part, Girard never tired of denouncing American doctors as charlatans, "ignorant jackasses," and "executioners of the human race." From Girard's point of view almost the worst crime committed by the doctors was the harm they did to commerce by frightening the population out of town when yellow fever returned in 1794, 1797, and 1798. He railed at preventive measures such as quarantine which interfered with trade, and declared that the only way of dealing with the fever was to take care of the sick, especially the sick poor. In his opinion it was fear that made people ill and the doctors rather than the disease that killed. After the epidemic of 1798 he wrote Jean Devèze that, of all the patients he had tended, "I do not suppose I cured one; nevertheless, you will agree with me that in my capacity as Physician of Philadelphia I have been very moderate and, that no one of my confreres has killed less than I."

Girard would be remembered as one of America's greatest philanthropists even if his work at Bush Hill were entirely forgotten. He provided financial assistance to the United States government during and after the War of 1812, when his generous subscriptions made possible the floating of a war loan and the establishment of the Second Bank of the United States. Girard's chief fame, however, came after his death in 1831 and as a result of the provisions of his will. Never before had an American bequeathed such a large estate to charitable and public purposes. A childless widower, at odds with his relatives, Girard made bequests to the city of Philadelphia for improvement of certain streets, to the state of Pennsylvania for development of canals, to the Masonic order to create a loan fund (and to cancel a debt owed to Girard), to the Pennsylvania Hospital, and to a number of philanthropic institutions and organizations in Philadelphia. The bulk of his estate he set aside (shades of Whitefield!) for founding a boarding school for poor, white, male orphan children. Girard's munificence set a high standard for later millionaires, some of whom, impressed by his example, persisted in establishing or endowing orphan homes many years after the need for such institutions was less pressing than it had been in Girard's day.

It is probable that Girard's interest in orphans dated back at least to the yellow-fever days. Certainly his palliative approach to philanthropy was as clearly revealed in the emergency of 1793 as was Rush's reformistic bent. Then, no less than in his later, more celebrated philanthropic bequests, Girard responded to specific needs rather than to general causes. Unlike Rush and other humanitarian reformers who came before and after him, Girard felt under no obligation to cure or prevent social disorders or to try to remold society by any means other than economic self-interest. Yet within the limits of a somewhat misanthropic philosophy, Girard, in times of emergency, was capable of acts of public usefulness and private kindness.

Rush and Girard are fair representatives of the two types of philanthropists the United States has produced. Their disparate interests and objectives point the directions American philanthropy was to follow through most of the nineteenth century.

III

Benevolence in the Young Republic

In the United States hardly anybody talks of the
beauty of virtue, but they maintain that virtue is
useful and prove it every day.

ALEXIS DE TOCQUEVILLE

Alexis de Tocqueville was twenty-five years old in the spring
of 1831 when he began a nine-months' journey through the
United States. The supposed purpose of the trip was to gather
material for a report on American prison systems. From the
outset, however, Tocqueville had a broader and bolder work in
mind. He was interested not only in prisons but, as he said, in
"all the mechanism of that vast American society which everyone talks of and nobody knows." In *Democracy in America*
(1835) Tocqueville had a good deal to say about the ways in
which Americans performed and justified acts of helpfulness to
one another, and on the effect of substantial equality of condition in producing mild and humane customs. The young
aristocrat was particularly impressed by the uncertain status

of the rich in a democratic society. The rich seemed to spring up daily from the multitude and almost as often to relapse into it again. Hence, Tocqueville said, there was no "race" of rich men in America. The rich did not form a distinct class, but were connected to the rest of the people by a thousand secret ties.

The strongest of those ties, or so it seems today, was the widespread acceptance of a common set of moral values and economic principles. These values and principles were better suited to the interests of the middle and lower classes than to the development of an aristocracy, for they justified the acquisition of wealth but condemned the display, enjoyment, waste, or hoarding of it. Few Americans seriously questioned the right of any man to get rich by personal effort, but a great many voiced endless concern about the uses to which wealth was put once it had been won. Democracy imposed or sought to impose, the same rules of conduct on the rich as on other members of society. In practice the rich often flouted convention, but the pervasive influence of custom and belief tended to hold them to middle-class standards of thrift, sobriety, and responsibility.

In view of the popular prejudice against ostentatious enjoyment of riches, the luxury of doing good was almost the only extravagance the American rich of the first half of the nineteenth century could indulge in with good consciences. Even the bequeathing of large estates to one's children was frowned on. A fortune left to children is a misfortune, declared Horace Mann, since it takes away the stimulus to effort, the restraints from indulgence, "the muscles out of the limbs, the brain out of the head, and virtue out of the heart." Mann, it must be admitted, had no fortune to bequeath; but his views were shared (although not rigidly adhered to) by the rich merchant and industrialist Amos Lawrence (1786–1852). Lawrence hailed his brother Abbott's gift of $50,000 to Harvard in 1847 in these words: "It enriches your descendants in a way that mere money never can do, and is a better investment than any you have ever made."

In an age of criticism and conscience, when vast fortunes were still a novelty, the methods by which wealth was acquired were scrutinized almost as carefully as the ways in which it was used. "They cheats one another and they calls that business," John Jacob Astor was reported to have said of the commercial classes of New York City. Emerson, who hoped and expected that the amelioration of society would come from the concessions of the rich rather than from the grasping of the poor, was discomfited by the discovery that the ways of trade were "selfish to the borders of theft, and supple to the borders, if not beyond the borders, of fraud." A Lowell physician, Dr. Joseph Curtis, advised the American Medical Association in 1849 that there was not a prison or reformatory in New England in which the hours of labor were as long, the time for meals as short, or ventilation as neglected as in the textile mills owned by Boston philanthropists. Thoreau, who remarked that philanthropy was the only virtue sufficiently appreciated by mankind, was not alone in thinking that "he who bestows the largest amount of time and money on the needy may be doing the most by his mode of life to produce the misery he strives in vain to relieve." Thus early Americans began to voice the suspicion that philanthropy was a device used by the rich to atone for their way of acquiring wealth.

Reasonable though the atonement theory of philanthropic motivation seems in the abstract, the diaries and private correspondence of pre–Civil War philanthropists betray no hints of feelings of guilt. On the contrary, these men seem to have been blandly confident that their prosperity came from God. Before retiring from business Amos Lawrence sometimes berated himself for "over-engagedness" in secular affairs; and Peter Chardon Brooks, an insurance broker and money lender who had amassed a million dollars by 1817, admitted that a self-made man was apt to value his money too highly and hug it too close. The major concern of such men, however, seems to have been to discharge the obligations of stewardship faithfully, so that, at the appointed hour, they might hear the joyful sound of "Well Done!" from the lips of their Divine Master. They gave out of a feeling of religious duty, because they frankly enjoyed giving, because some appeal touched their hearts, and because, as they frequently said, they thought giving for certain purposes was a good investment.

If proof of the complex motives of philanthropy were needed, it would be supplied by the variety of objects donors chose to support. Boston boasted—alas, in the literal sense— "such a number and combination of charities as has never before been found in any city of its size," and in almost every American community well-to-do citizens contributed to the founding and support of churches, hospitals, and orphanages. A breadline in New York, a cemetery in Morristown, New Jersey, a home for fallen but repentant women in Philadelphia, and a fund to assist young brides to set up housekeeping in the vicinity of Northampton, Massachusetts, all impressed their donors as proper objects of benevolence. Some of the most important gifts went to states or cities for public purposes: Girard left money for internal improvements in Philadelphia and Pennsylvania; Theodore Lyman won some sort of immortality by supplementing legislative appropriations for the Massachusetts state reformatory; and Thomas H. Perkins and Cyrus Butler, great men in their day, would be forgotten today save for their contributions toward the establishment of asylums for the blind and insane.

It is easy to laugh at the highly specialized and seemingly trivial purposes of many philanthropic activities. Yet who can deny, for example, that old people often suffer from failing eyesight? And who but Elias Boudinot, first president of the American Bible Society, was thoughtful enough to leave money in his will for purchasing spectacles for the aged poor? Amos Lawrence, having disengaged himself from business, rode out on fine days to distribute the tracts of the American Temperance Society and the Sunday School Union; on bad days he busied himself in selecting clothes, books, and other useful articles from storerooms in his house, bundled them into packages, and sent them off to needy students, professors, and clergymen. John Jacob Astor, not renowned for charitable giving, made an exception in favor of the Association for the Relief of Respectable Aged and Indigent Females. On the other hand, George Cheyne Shattuck, Boston's leading physician and a generous patron of education, passed up an opportunity to contribute to an old ladies' home; he preferred to give his money for such ends as the building of an observatory at his alma mater, Dartmouth. It was a halcyon day for philanthropists when a man could say, as the very rich and very generous William Appleton did in 1853, "I part with money in various ways of charity but much like to do it in my own way and not to be dictated to or even asked but in a general way, to give with others."

But giving with others was already a well-established feature

Benevolence in the Young Republic

of American philanthropy. The principle of voluntary association accorded so well with American political and economic theories that as early as 1820 the larger cities had an embarrassment of benevolent organizations. For the rest of the century, and even to our own day, one of the major problems of charity reformers would be to discover ways to co-ordinate the activities and fund drives of these competing agencies. In 1829 the economist and publisher, Mathew Carey, attempted—without much success—to interest Philadelphians in a single subscription campaign for the thirty-three benevolent societies then operating in the city. During the first half of the nineteenth century, societies for moral reform of individual sinners, and for the redemption and regeneration of a sinful world, multiplied even more rapidly than relief and aid organizations. As improvements in transportation and communication made it easier for people to join together, local societies merged into regional and then into national associations. William Ellery Channing, who disliked the substitution of the group for the individual conscience, remarked in 1829 that there was scarcely an object, good or bad, for whose advancement an association had not been formed.

The 1830's, an era of religious, political, and economic ferment, was the age of the "Benevolent Empire," a coalition of separate but closely related interdenominational religious societies. These various organizations collected and dispersed funds for distributing Bibles and religious tracts, for promoting foreign and home missions, for advancing the cause of temperance, Sabbath observance, and the Sunday-school movement; they supplied financial assistance to poor youths who wished to become clergymen and labored mightily to uplift the morals of seamen. Their combined membership ran into the hundreds of thousands and contributions to them amounted to several million dollars a year. Each of the societies held rousing national conventions and had officers, life-members, and, of course, rich angels. Elias Boudinot, Stephen Van Rensselaer, David Olyphant, Arthur and Lewis Tappan, and other philanthropists—usually although not always Federalist-Whig in their political leanings—took one or more of the societies to their bosoms, made generous contributions to their treasuries, and exerted a dominant influence on their policies and programs. In the hard times following the panic of 1837 many contributors had to curtail their gifts to the moral reform societies. The associations were further harassed by sectarian jealousies, by mounting sectional tensions, and by demands that they either denounce or defend the institution of slavery. The mission and tract societies adopted a policy of silence on the slavery issue, partly because it was politic to do so, and partly because (or so they maintained) their concern was with personal, not social, reform.

The American Colonization Society was founded (in 1817) about the same time as the moral reform societies and derived its support from approximately the same classes. Its work, which was the transporting of free Negroes to Africa, received the blessings of statesmen, the indorsement of state legislatures, and indirect assistance from the federal government. During the 1820's the Society raised enough money in the North and South to purchase land and found a struggling colony in Liberia. The Society managed to send a few hundred emigrants to the colony each year—a total of 11,000 by 1860 —but its operations proved a disappointment both to southerners, who seem to have expected it to rid the slave states of free Negroes, and to northerners who had hoped that the

Society would promote the manumission of slaves. After 1832, when William Lloyd Garrison denounced colonization as a scheme to strengthen slavery, the Society lost the support of the Tappans and other militant antislavery men. Its endeavors yielded such slight returns that critics labeled it "an American humane farce." Yet simply because it was *not* an antislavery organization it continued to receive contributions from conservative philanthropists such as James Beekman of New York and Robert Winthrop and Nathan Appleton of Boston. Appleton, a founder of the Massachusetts textile industry, and sensitively aware of the property rights of slaveowners, said in 1847 that he did not regard colonization as either an attack on or a solution to slavery. He supported the Colonization Society because he thought it was engaged in an experiment to ascertain whether the African race was fit for self-government and civilization.

At least some slaveowners were, or had been, prepared to go considerably farther than Appleton. The large number of free Negroes in Maryland and Virginia testified that hundreds of slaves had obtained freedom with the consent of their masters. After the 1830's legal restrictions made manumission more difficult to practice, but even so John McDonogh, a Louisiana planter and land speculator who conceived many ambitious philanthropies, allowed his slaves to use the proceeds of their labor over a fifteen-year period to buy their liberty. McDonogh sent his freed Negroes to Liberia, but John Randolph, in one of his several wills, conferred freedom on his four hundred slaves, valued at about a half-million dollars, and provided for their colonization in other parts of the United States. After a long legal battle the court carried out the terms of the will.

American Philanthropy

Few of the very rich were identified with the abolition movement before the mid-fifties. Among the exceptions were Arthur Tappan (1786–1865) and his brother Lewis (1788–1873). The Tappans, who attributed the success of their New York silk-importing business to moral supervision of their clerks and a strictly cash, one-price system of merchandising, came close to being caricatures of blue-nosed reformers. They worried about the "unchurched poor," the desecration of the Sabbath, and the use of wine in communion services. They founded a society to establish asylums for reformed prostitutes and, when that failed, organized a Society for Promoting the Observance of the Seventh Commandment. That the Tappans were pious busybodies cannot be denied, but they were also dedicated to the gospel of stewardship. They spent their wealth generously on religious and educational philanthropies, and when their championship of unpopular causes exposed them to the wrath of street mobs and the pressure of the business community, they faced their foes with uncommon courage. It was Arthur Tappan who secured William Lloyd Garrison's release from a Baltimore jail in 1830 by paying the fine and court costs imposed on him for libeling the owner of a vessel engaged in the domestic slave trade. As an alternative to colonization they proposed schemes for educating free Negroes for citizenship in the United States. They were among the organizers of the American Anti-Slavery Society in 1833, and active workers in the Society until it split in 1840. Thereafter, although somewhat reduced in influence because of Arthur's bankruptcy, they gave their support to the anti-Garrisonian political wing of the abolition movement.

Education, which loomed so large in the thought of the Tappans, also occupied a major share of the attention of other philanthropists. At the start of the century the provision of free schools for poor children was a favorite form of charity; but with the expansion and reform of the public school system philanthropists became active in endowing private academies for the children of the rich. The field of higher education, neglected by the federal government and very poorly supported by the states, gave philanthropists their greatest opportunity for service. A nation growing rapidly in population and wealth possibly needed more colleges than the twenty-odd in existence at the start of the century. As events proved, however, the nation did not require and could not support nearly all of the five hundred or more colleges that were founded between 1800 and 1860.

It would be logical to assume that supposedly practical Americans would have given first priority to the establishment of schools for engineers and technicians. In practice, however, they seem to have believed that the crying need was for institutions to train more clergymen and devout laymen. By 1830 twenty theological seminaries had been founded, with Andover, the seat of "sound, orthodox, Calvinistic principles of divinity" receiving particularly generous benefactions. Meanwhile, churches of all denominations organized a host of small colleges, many of which called themselves universities. Of all the new institutions, Amherst, founded by Congregationalists in 1821, seems to have been the pet of the philanthropists, largely because of its reputation as a feeder of ministerial students to the seminaries.

Promoters of colleges in the western states appealed to the East for financial assistance in much the same way that the colonial colleges had sought help from England. In their campaigns for funds they often claimed that the indoctrination of young westerners in sound moral principles was the best defense against the twin evils of religious indifference and political radicalism. The Tappans, who contributed to the founding of both Oberlin and Kenyon, thought that the solution to the financial problems of poor colleges and college students lay in attaching farms and workshops to classrooms. To this end they organized in 1831 a Society for Promoting Manual Training in Literary Institutions. The manual labor idea, although it furthered the founding of small schools, did not solve the needs of the larger and better established western colleges. After the depression of 1837 a number of these institutions, finding that frequent and competing solicitations increased the resistance of eastern philanthropists, formed the Society for Promotion of Collegiate and Theological Education in the West and, for a number of years, conducted a united fund drive.

The great increase in the number of colleges made it difficult for older institutions to attract and retain philanthropic support. Even Harvard, Unitarian since 1805, suffered from the competition of younger but more religiously orthodox colleges. Bostonians had contributed slightly more than a quarter of a million dollars to Harvard between 1800 and 1830; in the next fifteen years, while raising $330,000 for Amherst, they gave but $84,000 to Harvard. Beginning in the late 1840's, however, and increasingly in the 1850's, Harvard began to receive the gifts of Abbott Lawrence, Samuel Appleton, and other industrialists. Numerous institutions were favored by the families or individuals whose names they bore or adopted, but in at least one instance, Rutgers, college authorities made the mistake of renaming the institution in honor of a prospective benefactor who failed to make the expected princely donation.

Benevolence in the Young Republic

On the other hand, a public lecture by Mark Hopkins, the president of Williams College, made such a favorable impression on Amos Lawrence that the philanthropist made a large unsolicited gift to the college and followed his initial donation with several more.

The federal government was the recipient of another unsolicited and quite unprecedented gift in the form of James Smithson's bequest of approximately $500,000. Smithson, a British chemist who died in 1829, left his fortune to a nephew with the proviso that if the latter died without issue (as he obligingly did) the entire estate should pass "to the United States of America to found at Washington, under the name of the Smithsonian Institution, an establishment for the increase and diffusion of knowledge among men." Upon the death of the nephew in 1835 Congress debated the constitutionality and propriety of accepting the gift, John C. Calhoun opposing and John Quincy Adams favoring acceptance. As President, Adams had been unsuccessful in his efforts to expand the activities of the federal government in education and research; now, however, he was not to be denied, and in 1836 Congress voted to accept the bequest. Not until ten years later, after further controversy and debate, and after the loss of the original gift through unwise investment (Congress appropriated $500,000 to cover the loss) did "the establishment" at last come into being. Adams again played an important role in securing approval of the act that set up the Institution, but it remained for Joseph Henry, the brilliant physicist who served as director of the Smithsonian from its founding in 1846 until his death more than thirty years later, to establish research and publication as the means by which the Institution was to carry out its mission of increasing and diffusing knowledge among men.

While Congress was still debating what to do with the Smithson gift, another institute for disseminating knowledge opened in Boston. The donor, John Lowell, retired from business after the death of his wife and two young daughters and spent the rest of his brief life in restless travel through Europe and the Middle East. Shortly before his death in 1836 he put his will into final shape, directing that a sum of $250,000 be used to found the Lowell Institute. Lowell stipulated that the endowment, instead of being spent on buildings, should be used to sponsor public lectures to instruct the people of Boston in science, literature, history, and religion. Although imparting more knowledge to serious-minded Bostonians might seem like carrying coals to Newcastle, the Institute opened in 1840 with a series of lectures on geology by Benjamin Silliman. Through a policy of generous remuneration the Institute was able to bring to its platforms some of the foremost men of letters and science of both the old and new worlds.

Beginning in the 1840's, as the founding of Lowell Institute and the Smithsonian Institution suggest, scientific research and intellectual inquiry—as opposed to moral instruction and reform—began to figure more prominently as objects of American philanthropy. Louis Agassiz, who came to the United States to lecture at Lowell Institute, remained to become professor of zoology and geology at Harvard. There his work was supported by the gifts of Abbott Lawrence, Francis Gray, and other Boston capitalists as well as by grants from the Massachusetts legislature. Agassiz's insatiable requirements for funds for his museum of comparative zoology gave philanthropists an object lesson in the cost of scientific research. At about the same time, by founding Cooper Union in New York City, Peter Cooper (1791–1883) continued the Franklin tradition of advancing science and art "in their application to the varied and useful purposes of life." George Peabody (1795–1869), the American-born banker who lived in London after 1837, made it possible for his countrymen to display their industries and inventions at the Crystal Palace Exhibition of 1851 and through his gift of the Peabody Institute enriched Baltimore's cultural life with an art gallery, lecture hall, and conservatory of music. Peabody's and Henry Grinnell's underwriting of the expenses of polar expeditions during the 1850's popularized geographical exploration as an object of philanthropic support. Similarly, the bequest of John Jacob Astor, which established the Astor Library in New York, and the gifts of Joshua Bates for the founding of the Boston Public Library in 1852, presaged what was to become one of the standard forms of philanthropy in the second half of the nineteenth century.

Promoters of two patriotic undertakings met difficulty in raising money for objects that would, offhand, seem to have had popular appeal. The Bunker Hill Monument Association of Boston ran out of money and into debt three years after laying the cornerstone of the monument in 1825. Construction had to be suspended for almost a decade. The obelisk was not completed until the 1840's, after Amos Lawrence and Judah Touro of New Orleans had each contributed $10,000 and a "Ladies Fair" had raised $30,000 for the project. Meanwhile, the Washington National Monument Society, founded in 1833, sought subscriptions for a memorial to George Washington in the national capital. More than fifty years passed before the beautiful shaft was finished, for although the Society had collected enough money to begin construction in 1848, funds were exhausted by 1855, and for many years thereafter efforts to obtain additional support from private citizens or the federal government yielded disappointing returns. Partisan feelings and, in the case of the Washington Monument, religious considerations were partly responsible for the indifference and even hostility to these undertakings. But more important was the fact that the sense of national patriotism was still comparatively weak in pre–Civil War America, despite Fourth of July orations and the vogue of eulogistic biographies and histories.

In contrast to the lagging support accorded patriotic monuments, Americans gave enthusiastically and liberally for foreign relief. In the 1820's volunteer committees arranged balls, fairs, auctions, debating contests, and theatrical benefits to raise money for the cause of Greek independence. The committees employed nearly all the devices of modern charity drives to levy contributions for Greek relief from merchants, shippers, laborers, and school children, and brought a number of Greek war orphans to this country for adoption. In the autumn of 1832, when the starving people of Cape Verde Islands rowed out to a ship hoping to buy food, they were astonished to learn that the vessel had been sent from the United States for the express purpose of relieving their necessities. Individuals and churches in New England, Philadelphia, and New York had heard of their need and had raised thousands of dollars for their assistance. Boston gentlemen sent a relief ship to the Madeira Islands in 1843 and were rewarded when appreciative islanders sent the ship back laden with casks of choice old Madeira. The Irish famine of 1846–47, the worst calamity of the entire period, called forth the largest and most widely shared response from the American people. New York's merchant prince, A. T. Stewart, and other Irish-Americans showed sympathy in abundance, but generosity cut across national and religious lines. To carry the contributions of Massachusetts alone required two sloops of war, four merchant ships, and two steamers. It was both fitting and ironic that the Boston bluebloods, Josiah Quincy and Robert Winthrop, the latter an Episcopalian descendant of Puritan John Winthrop, should have taken leading parts in organizing relief efforts for the distressed people of Catholic Ireland.

American readiness to assist the unfortunate in foreign lands seemed to bear out Tocqueville's view that democracy, by destroying barriers of class and privilege, fostered a general feeling of compassion for all members of the human race. But in the 1830's and 40's thoughtful Americans were less concerned about the consequences of democracy than about the work that remained to be done for its realization. There was need, said William Ellery Channing in 1841, for "vigorous efforts, springing from love, sustained by faith" for diffusing knowledge, self-respect, self-control, morality and religion through all classes of the population. At the time these were the areas in which philanthropy was most interested and best fitted to serve.

IV

Saints and Scolds

What is it we heartily wish of each other? Is it to be pleased and flattered? No, but to be convicted and exposed, to be shamed out of our nonsense of all kinds. . . .

RALPH WALDO EMERSON

With some exceptions, like the Tappans, contributions to moral reform and gifts to the unfortunate involved few sacrifices by donors. Not even the Tappans insisted that the rich should give away all they possessed, and Amos Lawrence once reflected that the more he gave the more he seemed to have. Some men, like Girard, gave up their money only after death; others, like Lawrence, gave liberally of their income during life but made no significant charitable bequests. "I have given in my lifetime what I felt it was my duty to give," Edward Delavan, the angel of the temperance movement, said in his will. "I think my family is entitled to what is left of my estate." Generally speaking, philanthropists made their contributions out of surplus wealth and stopped giving whenever they thought it prudent to do so.

To some guardians of conscience neither the ends nor the means of conventional giving warranted the name of philanthropy. Emerson, in "Self-Reliance" (1841), warned the "foolish philanthropist" not to come to his door begging for "your miscellaneous popular charities; the education at colleges of fools; the building of meeting-houses to the vain end to which many now stand; alms to sots, and the thousandfold Relief Societies." Thoreau scorned "a charity which dispenses the crumbs that fall from its overloaded tables, which are left after its feasts!" He wondered at the boasts of men who gave one-tenth of their income to charity while keeping nine-tenths for themselves; and he asked whether such a distribution was to be explained by the generosity of the givers or by "the remissness of the officers of justice."

There were a number of philanthropists in the pre–Civil War period, however, who were as little impressed by the common run of charities as Emerson, who were as alert as Thoreau to inhumane social practices, and who offered more than passive resistance to injustice. These reformer-philanthropists conducted a general inquest into the abuses of their time and were more than willing to point out better ways of doing things. Not all the causes they championed were unpopular, but they did have to contend with complacency, and, at times, sentimentality. Mainly it was inertia—passive good will combined with prejudice against change and reform— rather than active opposition that they encountered. The vehemence of their agitation shocked persons of milder temperaments and easier consciences. Their peculiarities, prejudices, and blind spots are all too apparent, as are the inadequacies of some of the remedies they proposed. They were neither revolutionaries nor visionaries, and perhaps were not much more sensitive to wrong than ordinary men and women; but they had a much stronger than ordinary sense of personal responsibility for ending or mitigating wrongs. They became excited about issues in which their own interests were not involved, and they had the energy and daring to carry their feelings into action.

The miscellaneous popular charities whose numbers increased during the hard times of 1816–21, and in each succeeding depression, were among the principal targets of the reformers. The trouble with such agencies, in the opinion of Joseph Tuckerman (1778–1840) of Boston and John Griscom (1774–1840) of New York, two of the most influential of the charity reformers, was that while relieving the sentiments of the comfortable classes, they did more harm than good to the poor. The American charity reformers, like their British and Continental counterparts with whom they were in frequent communication, were obsessed by a fear of pauperism. They wanted to help the poor but were so fearful of pauperizing them that the only commodity they dared offer was advice. That they gave liberally: hints on household management, admonitions on waste, intemperance, and idleness, and sermons on the virtues of self-help.

Individualistic and moralistic in outlook though the charity reformers were, they were not as naïve as they sometimes seem. Tuckerman, Griscom, and their associates put in motion schemes for the spread of savings banks, life insurance, and benefit societies among the poor; and in the course of their attack on pauperism they lent support to a host of reform movements. The material as well as the moral state of the poor

Amos Lawrence. (From Freeman Hunt, *Lives of American Merchants*, New York: Derby & Jackson, 1858.)

"Please Sir, May I Have a Bed." Newsboys' Lodging House of Children's Aid Society of New York, 1854. (From Charles Loring Brace, *The Dangerous Classes of New York*, New York: Wynkoop & Hallenbeck, 1872.)

engaged the attention of Robert M. Hartley (1796–1881), who founded the New York Association for Improving the Condition of the Poor in 1843 and managed it for the next three decades. Under Hartley's leadership the A.I.C.P. devoted part of its energies to "incidental labors" for social betterment, particularly in the fields of housing, sanitation, and child welfare.

Although suspicious of unwise private charity, the reformers were even more critical of public poor relief. Tuckerman urged repeal of existing poor laws and abolition of all public assistance except that furnished in closely supervised institutions. England attempted a revision of her poor laws along these lines in 1834, but public opinion in the United States (where the votes of the poor counted more at the polls) would not accept such a drastic step. Nevertheless during the 1820's legislatures in several states ordered investigations of prevailing methods of poor relief. The reports of the investigating committees confirmed the reformers' charges that some of the poor were maintained in their own homes at the taxpayers' expense; others, however, were either farmed out to contractors at a stipulated price or "sold" to the person who bid the lowest sum for keeping them. Since the bidders themselves were often desperately poor, the money paid them for keeping paupers constituted a kind of relief— "a species of economy" (said the New York report) "much boasted of by some of our town officers." With rare unanimity the reports indorsed the almshouse or poor farm—utilized by the more populous communities for a century or more—as the most humane and economical method of caring for paupers. A well-regulated institution, such as the one at Poughkeepsie, New York, employed its inmates at picking oakum, washing, spinning, cooking, and farm work, and fed and clothed each at an annual cost of twenty-five dollars. "Our house of industry," reported the gratified managers, "affords an opportunity to economize, and to support our paupers at least 50 per cent less than formerly."

The reformers were more successful in inducing communities to build almshouses than in policing them once they had been established. The poorhouses founded in the 1820's and 30's soon become catchalls for victims of every variety of misery, misfortune, and misconduct. The old and the young, the vagrant and the abandoned, the feeble-minded, insane, and disabled, were all herded together in buildings that were poorly constructed, foully maintained, and wretchedly furnished. "Common domestic animals are usually more humanely provided for than the paupers in some of these institutions" was the verdict of one investigatory commission at mid-century. In New York in the 1850's a committee of the State Senate found evidence of such "filth, nakedness, licentiousness, . . . and . . . gross neglect of the most ordinary comforts and decenies of life" that it forbore to publish its findings in detail lest the report disgrace the State.

The children in prison rather than those in pauper asylums first aroused the sympathy of nineteenth-century reformers. John Griscom, representing the New York Society for the Prevention of Pauperism, and Thomas Eddy, who had been active in prison reform movements since the 1790's, worked for five years after 1819 to get youthful offenders out of jails and into reformatories. Through their efforts the New York House of Refuge, the first reformatory for juvenile delinquents in the United States, was founded in 1825. Shortly afterward, Philadelphia, traditionally the center of American prison reform activities, built a similar House of Refuge; and Boston, under the prodding of Mayor Josiah Quincy, soon established a House of Reformation which, in the opinion of informed students might have served as a model for all correctional institutions. The success of the Boston House of Reformation led Theodore Lyman in the 1840's to make gifts totaling almost $75,000 for the establishment of the first state juvenile reformatory at Westborough, Massachusetts.

While other humanitarians were demanding special institutions for wayward youth, Charles Loring Brace (1826-90), a twenty-seven-year-old city missionary in the Five Points district of New York, developed a comprehensive program for combatting delinquency at its source. The New York Children's Aid Society, organized by Brace in 1853, provided religious meetings, workshops, industrial schools, and lodging houses for the poorest and most neglected children of the metropolis. Brace, who regarded these undisciplined and often homeless youngsters as menaces to society, described the Children's Aid Society as "a moral and physical disinfectant." He was particularly interested in the possibility of "draining" New York of destitute children. Beginning in 1854 the Children's Aid Society annually sent hundreds of boys and girls to foster homes in the West. The success of the emigration scheme rested in part on the demand for unpaid farm labor. To Brace this circumstance did not lessen the charity of those who gave poor children homes in return for work. Brace, like Cotton Mather, believed the best charity that could be offered the idle was an opportunity to work, and he was convinced that boys and girls were better off in Christian homes, especially farm homes, than in any institution.

Brace's informal placement methods set off a long controversy. Roman Catholics complained that Catholic children were being sent to Protestant homes; westerners protested that the Children's Aid Society was filling western jails and reformatories with petty criminals; and welfare workers objected that the Society did not carefully scrutinize the homes in which it placed children. Brace investigated the charges, modified his methods, and persisted in his labors for almost forty years. His work did much to popularize foster-home care for dependent children as opposed to institutionalization, and his preventive "child-saving" approach, adopted at a time when so much emphasis was placed on correctional or reformatory methods, exercised a wholesome influence on later development in child welfare.

The founding of juvenile reformatories was part of the larger movement for prison reform. In the United States this movement went back at least to 1776 when a Society for Alleviating the Miseries of Public Prisons had been organized in Philadelphia. By the 1820's, after half a century of experience in substitution of confinement for corporal punishment, two rival systems of prison discipline had emerged: the Pennsylvania or "separate" plan used at the great and costly Eastern State Penitentiary at Cherry Hill; and the Auburn, or "congregate" system developed in New York State. In the former, inmates lived, worked, ate, and slept in solitary cells; under the Auburn plan prisoners were locked up alone at night, but worked and ate together during the day, theoretically in absolute silence and subject to harsh punishment for breaking rules against communicating with one another.

Each of the methods had staunch advocates. The Pennsylvania system appealed to humanitarians because of the supposed penitential benefits of solitary confinement, while the

Auburn plan found support among persons impressed by its demonstrated economy. Auburn won the indorsement of the influential Boston Prison Discipline Society, which, under the leadership of Louis Dwight, a former agent of the Tract and Bible Societies, issued propaganda for adoption of the congregate system throughout the nation. On the other hand Samuel Gridley Howe, Horace Mann, Charles Sumner, and many other reformers remained partisans of the Pennsylvania system. The dispute produced a spate of pamphlets, the most valuable of which was Dorothea Dix's *Remarks on Prisons and Prison Discipline* (1845), and Nathaniel Hawthorne made a visionary prison reformer the villain of *The Blithedale Romance* (1852). In the heat of the controversy legislatures and prison administrators initiated reforms in the construction and management of penitentiaries which for a brief period made American prisons rank among the most progressive in the world.

In the long run it proved impossible to maintain interest in prison reform at the high level necessary to effect lasting improvement. Other issues intervened, and reformers soon found prison discipline a less interesting subject of debate and speculation than projects for preventing crime. Before interest had cooled, however, a New York Quaker, Isaac Hopper (1771–1852), had begun his work of helping discharged prisoners find homes and jobs. Meanwhile in Boston a shoemaker named John Augustus (1785–1859) voluntarily assumed and performed the duties of probation officer. Over a period of almost twenty years Augustus devoted the earnings of his shop and applied the contributions of well-wishers to bailing and rehabilitating drunkards and persons convicted of petty crimes. Necessarily selective in the bestowal of assistance, since his resources were limited, he nevertheless helped many unfortunates who were "undeserving" by conventional standards. Augustus was "extraordinarily given to help the helpless and love the unlovely," said the radical preacher, Theodore Parker. "Ministers preach benevolence and beneficence—he *went* and *did* it."

Three more famous philanthropists, among the most justly celebrated America has produced, also *went* and *did* acts of extraordinary usefulness to classes previously neglected and often deemed beyond help. The Reverend Thomas Hopkins Gallaudet (1787–1851), Dr. Samuel Gridley Howe (1801–76), and Dorothea Dix (1802–87) were not specially qualified by training for the service which won their fame. They abandoned their intended careers in order to help deaf mutes and the blind, and to rescue the insane from cages in jails and almshouses. Gallaudet, a graduate of Andover Theological Seminary, demonstrated to the nation that deaf mutes could be educated. He founded the first American school for the deaf, gained support for this work from private donors, state legislatures, and even Congress, and lived to see state schools for the deaf widely established. Howe's special field was instruction of the blind, and his most celebrated feat was teaching Laura Bridgman—blind, deaf, and mute—the use of language and a variety of manual skills. But before Howe became a teacher of the blind in the 1830's, he had fought in the Greek War of Independence and administered relief to Greek civilians; and long after he won renown as head of Perkins Institution, he plunged into other causes, and embarked on new crusades to educate the feeble-minded and teach the mute to speak. Howe was a latter-day Benjamin Rush in the multiplicity of his interests, in his love of liberty, aptitude for controversy, and unquenchable optimism. Even oysters, he said, were capable of improvement!

As for Dorothea Dix, her career offers one of the best examples the nineteenth century affords of sustained and constructive agitation for humanitarian reform. She was not a pioneer in the field of better treatment of the insane. Much had already been accomplished when she began her work. Several reputable hospitals for the mentally ill had been founded by incorporated bodies; John McLean and other donors had given money for improving and expanding facilities for the insane, and a number of states had opened publicly supported asylums. Nearly all of these institutions made at least nominal provision for caring for the dependent insane at low cost. So much progress seemed to have been made in the years just before Miss Dix's investigations that there was danger, not that her proposals would seem outlandish, but that further action and expenditure for the insane might seem superfluous. Dorothea Dix's task was the difficult one of puncturing complacency, indicating omissions, specifying mistakes and abuses, and stirring the public conscience to greater exertions.

Like another great agitator, Anthony Benezet, Miss Dix was a teacher by profession. Largely self-taught, she had conducted a successful school for daughters of Boston's leading families and had tutored the children of her friend and pastor, William Ellery Channing. In the winter of 1841, somewhat at loose ends following a long illness, she agreed to teach a Sunday-school class for women prisoners in the East Cambridge jail. Here she found insane women locked in unheated cells. Anyone might have done what she then did. She petitioned the court for warmer quarters for these women. But Dorothea Dix was not content to stop there. She made it her business to find out how the insane were cared for in the rest of Massachusetts. After two years she was ready to report her findings in a *Memorial to the Legislature of Massachusetts* (1843), a document which proved that Victorian decorum was not inconsistent with the presentation of sordid social truths.

"I proceed, gentlemen," Miss Dix began, "briefly to call your attention to the *present* state of insane persons confined within the Commonwealth, in *cages, closets, cellars, stalls, pens; chained, naked, beaten with rods,* and *lashed* into obedience." Armed with facts, figures, names, places, and dates, she cited instance after instance of the mistreatment or neglect of the mentally ill. Poor-law officials, as she pointed out, found it cheaper to "lodge" the pauper insane in jails and almshouses than to send them to asylums. In any case, the number of dependent insane and idiotic persons was at least twice as large as the total capacity of the three asylums in the state. Fortunately she had friends as well as facts at her disposal. Horace Mann lent his assistance, and Samuel Gridley Howe was chairman of the legislative committee to which the *Memorial* was referred. Howe's committee indorsed both the findings and conclusions of her investigation and secured passage of a bill enlarging the Worcester Asylum to provide more space for poor patients.

Massachusetts was the first phase of a forty-year campaign that took Miss Dix throughout the United States, into Canada, Scotland, England, Italy, and Turkey, and spread her influence as far as Japan. It would be incorrect to imply that she single-handedly worked a revolution in the care of the insane. Yet it is true that her "sad, patient, deliberate" investigations resulted in the founding of many new state hospitals and at least a temporary improvement in the treatment of the mentally ill. Wherever she went her methods were essentially the same: inquiry and research to determine the facts about the number and condition of the insane; efforts to arouse public opinion through articles in the press and memorials to the legislature; and cultivation of powerful figures in and out of public office. She professed a lady-like repugnance of politics, but she had a real talent for political maneuver. She knew when to sprinkle her humanitarian pleas with the salt of economy and often concluded her appeals by observing that "it is cheaper to take charge of the insane in a curative institution than to support them elsewhere for life." She was adept at discovering the most influential men in legislatures and in bringing them into her camp. The men she feared most were not those who openly opposed her but those who said they sympathized with her aims, wept over her reports, and then found compelling, noble reasons for steeling their hearts against compassion.

Such a man was President Franklin Pierce, at whose hands Miss Dix suffered one of her few major defeats. In 1848 she sent a *Memorial* to Congress in which she estimated that not more than one-twelfth of the insane population of the country could be accommodated in existing hospitals and asylums. As a means of dealing with the problem she proposed federal assistance in financing care of the insane through land grants to the states. Grants of this sort had frequently been made for education and internal improvements, and, on two occasions, for schools for the deaf. In 1854, after six years of lobbying by Miss Dix, both houses of Congress passed her bill. It apportioned 12,225,000 acres of public land among the states for the support of insane asylums and institutions for the deaf.

President Pierce, professing regret for having to do so, vetoed the bill. He acknowledged that the duty of providing for those who suffered from want and disease of body or mind was "among the highest and holiest" of human obligations, but he said he feared the effect of Miss Dix's bill would be "prejudicial rather than beneficial to the noble offices of charity," since it would dry up the normal springs of benevolence. "If Congress have the power to make provision for the indigent insane . . . ," he warned, "it has the same power to provide for the indigent who are not insane; and thus to transfer to the Federal Government the charge of all poor in all the states." For his part, continued Pierce, "I cannot find any authority in the Constitution for making the Federal Government the great almoner of public charity throughout the United States."

Of course Miss Dix and her supporters were not asking the federal government to play such a role, or to assume exclusive responsibility for all the poor in all the states. They wanted only to have a portion of the public lands granted to the states to enable them to fulfill their obligations better than they were then able. But to Pierce principle was more important than policy, and his principle, as a critic has remarked, was that no power that might be abused should be used. Yet Pierce sensed the implications of the Dix bill accurately. Had it become law, not only the care of the insane but all public welfare programs might have developed quite differently. As it was the United States had to wait another eighty years before the federal government began to assist and strengthen state programs for certain categories of needy persons.

To Horace Mann (1796–1859) and some other friends of Miss Dix, Howe, and Gallaudet, the improvement of common schools for normal children seemed an even more urgent matter than the establishment of institutions for the afflicted. No nineteenth-century reform movement had a broader base than the crusade for good schools, and none was expected to yield greater benefits. The educational reformers maintained that raising the general level of culture through more and better schools was the only sure way of accomplishing a thoroughgoing reform of society. A nation which made education freely available to all would not neglect its unfortunate members; it would not have to bear the burdens of pauperism, crime, immorality, and intemperance; and it would be prepared to meet social crises with wisdom and humanity.

The task of the reformers, however, was not to praise education, which nearly everybody did, but to obtain adequate financial support for it. They did not ask free schools for the poor, since both private philanthropists and public authorities were ready to provide that. They wanted free, public, entirely tax-supported education for all children—rich, poor, and middling—without any stigma of charity attached to it. The story of their struggle to win this objective lies outside the realm of the history of philanthropy, and yet it involves the difficult problem of the relationship of philanthropy to reform. Theoretically, philanthropy pioneers, proves the value of a service, then allows the community or the state to assume responsibility for the task, and moves on to some new field. In practice, as in the public school controversy when societies operating charity schools presented one of the numerous obstacles to the establishment of tax-supported educational systems, philanthropy may become a vested interest and display no eagerness to surrender its prerogatives. Fortunately there are philanthropists and philanthropists, and no one would deny that title to Horace Mann, the lawyer, politician, bureaucrat, college president, and reformer.

Mann had been a poor boy who studiously observed the maxims of self-help in his own career, and he preached those maxims with less humor and even more zeal than Benjamin Franklin. It was characteristic of him to find Richard Henry Dana's *Two Years before the Mast* deficient in statistics, wanting in moral lessons, and too full of descriptions. But Mann's earnestness and seriousness were well suited to his time and purpose, and he revealed in all his works a dedication to great ends. He was a figure of some prominence in Massachusetts politics when, in 1837, he accepted the relatively minor post of secretary of the State Board of Education. His long tenure in this office gave him an opportunity to canvass every shortcoming in the existing school system and to promote improvements in instruction, discipline, curriculum, textbooks, and the training of teachers. His *Annual Reports*, each as carefully prepared as a legal brief and as hortatory as a sermon, aroused interest and controversy not only in Massachusetts but in nearly every other state.

Like Howe and other humanitarian reformers of his day Mann found in phrenology an apparent scientific justification for his belief in the improvability and infinite educability of the human race. He had unbounded faith in the practical uses of education, particularly in overcoming poverty. But it was the common welfare rather than individual success that excited him, and it was the religious doctrine of stewardship much more than scientific rationalism that guided his thought. He believed that property owners were indebted to the social intelligence of preceding generations for their wealth and that they were therefore obligated to use it to transmit the common body of knowledge to future generations through schools. He was disappointed that rich men contributed little beyond their taxes to public education. When Abbott Lawrence, in making a gift of $50,000 to Harvard, said, "Elementary education appears to be well provided for in Massachusetts," Mann replied that salaries for women teachers in the public schools averaged $68.40 for the entire school term and that the average number of books in school libraries was twenty-five. In his last *Annual Report* he took a hard look at Massachusetts' latest wonder, the reform school at Westborough. "One tenth part of its cost," said Mann, "would have done more in the way of prevention than its whole amount can accomplish in the way of reclaiming."

In 1848, convinced that a man or child must be free before he could be educated, Mann gave up his official post and re-entered politics on an antislavery platform. During the 1850's, in response to the Fugitive Slave Law, the Kansas-Nebraska Act, and the struggle for Kansas, other reformers also put the cause of the Negro above their earlier interests. Miss Dix was an exception to the general rule because she, in order not to jeopardize her usefulness to the insane, refused to become involved in the sectional controversy. But Howe, as impetuous in full-bearded middle-age as in his Byronic youth, flung himself wholeheartedly into the abolition movement. Charles Sumner, the foremost peace orator of the 1840's, was anything but pacifistic in his utterances about slavery and slaveholders in the 1850's, and Gerrit Smith, a generous contributor to the peace movement, had concluded by the late 1850's that there was no possibility of ending slavery by peaceful means. Smith gave financial assistance to John Brown and was so deeply implicated in Brown's plans for direct action against slavery that he became temporarily insane after the debacle at Harpers Ferry. Theodore Parker and a few other clergymen, not content to denounce slavery from the pulpit, enrolled in Vigilance Committees which raised funds to speed fugitives to Canada or pay for the legal defense of Negroes held under the Fugitive Slave law. Prominent lawyers offered their services free of charge or at nominal costs as counsel to fugitives, and philanthropists who had once given money to colonize Negroes in Africa now contributed funds to send white settlers to Kansas. Amos Lawrence's son discharged his obligation of stewardship by paying for rifles shipped to the free-soil settlers.

If philanthropy means spending time and effort and risking personal safety to aid the down trodden, the ranks of pre–Civil War philanthropists must be broadened to include the men and women who violated federal laws to shelter fugitives, as well as those who raided the South to rescue or abduct slaves. Levi Coffin, reputed head of the Underground Railway, is said to have assisted about one hundred fugitives a year over a period of more than thirty years. The intrepid Harriet Tubman, herself a fugitive, repeatedly returned to the South to lead her fellows to freedom. Some who engaged in this dangerous work paid a heavy price. John Brown sacrificed not only his own life but those of two of his sons. Reverend Charles Torrey, who resigned from a Providence pulpit to work for abolition, died in a southern jail for his efforts. Calvin Fairbanks spent more than seventeen years in prison in Kentucky as punishment for abducting slaves and, according to his own account, received something like 35,000 lashes at the hands of his jailers. One Rush R. Sloane of Sandusky, Ohio paid a fine of $3,000 for assisting fugitives to Canada, while

Thomas Garrett of Wilmington, Delaware, convicted of numerous breaches of the Fugitive Slave law, surrendered all his property in payment of fines totaling $8,000. This doughty old Quaker, undeterred by his punishment, continued to give aid and comfort to refugees until 1861. "The war came a little too soon for my business," he said. "I wanted to help off three thousand slaves. I had only got up to 2,700."

The Civil War came too soon for all the philanthropists. None of their work was finished and parts of it were hardly begun when the fighting started, bringing new opportunities for service.

V

Civil War Philanthropies

Long, too long America,
Traveling roads all even and peaceful you learn'd
   from joys and prosperity only,
But now, ah now, to learn from crises of an-
   guish . . .
And now to conceive and show to the world what
   your children en-masse really are, . . .

WALT WHITMAN

The first need of the Civil War was for men to fight it; the next was for civilians to support and succor the armies; and the third was for marshaling material and spiritual resources into an overpowering will to victory. In April, 1861, neither the North nor the South anticipated a struggle of the magnitude and duration that in fact took place. Both parties looked, as Lincoln said in his Second Inaugural Address, "for an easier triumph, and a result less fundamental and astounding." Throughout the war, patriots on each side, from Lincoln and Davis down, complained of laxity, indifference, self-seeking, and internal opposition that weakened war efforts. Yet from the very beginning the war roused the charitable energies and impulses of the American people, and of American women in particular, as they had never been aroused before. Charitable enterprises were of great importance, not only in providing needed supplies and services to the troops, but in building up civilian morale and the will to win.

"The uprising of the women of the land" (as the Reverend Henry W. Bellows, chairman of the United States Sanitary Commission called the phenomenon) began on the day Lincoln summoned 75,000 militia to meet the challenge of Fort Sumter. Women in several New England cities, soon followed by others from New York to Iowa and California, organized to aid soldiers and their families. Before the war ended something like 15,000 soldiers' aid societies had been founded and almost every Northern home had been canvassed for funds and supplies. One of the first women to volunteer for more onerous duties, and almost the last to leave the field, was Dorothea Dix. Although nearing sixty, she presented herself at the War Department in the first week of the war and shortly thereafter accepted the post of Superintendent of Female Nurses. Miss Dix's specifications for female nurses—and she was not one to relax her standards—were mature years, good health, and plainness in person and dress. "No bows, no curls, no jewelry, and no hoop-skirts," she decreed.

With or without Miss Dix's approval, for her authority was challenged by the Medical Bureau of the Army, an estimated thirty-two hundred women served as nurses with Union forces. Among them were six hundred Roman Catholic nuns, frowned upon by Miss Dix, but highly esteemed by the troops and hospital surgeons. More to the superintendent's liking were the three Woolsey sisters, daughters of the president of

Yale, and Katharine Prescott Wormeley, whose father was a British admiral. Illness cut short Louisa May Alcott's career as a nurse, but she served long enough to gather material for *Hospital Sketches* (1863), her first successful book. Most of the regular female nurses served in hospitals behind the lines, but "Mother" Mary Ann Bickerdyke, once a student at Oberlin and an herb-doctor at the start of the war, worked with such devotion and efficiency in battle zones that she became one of the authentic heroes of the war. Harriet Tubman, following Massachusetts troops to the South, mingled hospital chores with scouting and spying behind enemy lines. After every important battle free-lance "reliefers" and nurses hastened to the field. The most celebrated and ubiquitous of these independent operators was Clara Barton (1821–1912). A former teacher and Patent Office clerk, Miss Barton displayed her genius for obtaining relief supplies and getting them promptly to places of need long before she succeeded in organizing the American Red Cross. The prestige she gained through her war work helped in the later undertaking.

In zeal for war relief the women of the Confederacy equaled their sisters in the North. They organized hundreds of aid associations and during the first year of the war assumed almost complete responsibility for clothing southern troops. Soldiers on their way to or from the front found hospitality, entertainment, and medical service in Wayside Inns maintained by volunteers. Nursing appealed as strongly to southern as to northern women. They took battle casualties into their homes, and after Gettysburg some of them were permitted to go to the battlefield to tend their wounded. In 1862 the "petticoat gunboat" fever struck the Confederacy; in state after state women took collections at prayer meetings and Sunday schools, and held fairs, bazaars, raffles, and concerts to raise money to build gunboats. In the South, as in the North, there were drives for gifts to widows and orphans of war heroes. Southern sympathies and pocketbooks seem to have been particularly susceptible to appeals for the relief of families of men killed either in defense of the flag of the Confederacy or in pulling down the emblem of the Union.

Measured by money expended, the largest charitable efforts, North and South, were devoted to relieving families of service men. Oft-repeated warnings of the dangers of unwise giving were forgotten for the moment as community and state-wide relief organizations solicited contributions from farmers, merchants, railroad companies, factory owners, and workers, and showered gifts on the needy. Local, county, and state aid in the form of enlistment bounties and direct relief to dependent families seems to have been even more bountiful. Wartime generosity brought increased public debt and higher taxes, factors which had considerable bearing on the revival of hostility to public poor relief in the postwar years.

Religious charities flourished on both sides of the battle lines. "Both read the same Bible, and pray to the same God; and each invokes His aid against the other," mused Lincoln in 1864. The Bible Society of the Confederacy, with some assistance from the American Bible Society, labored to collect Bibles and testaments for distribution to southern soldiers; and the Evangelical Tract Society of Petersburg, Virginia published a religious paper and kept rebel troops well supplied with tracts against swearing, drinking, and gambling. In the North, the work of the Christian Commission was generously supported by the evangelical churches, the Young Men's Christian Associations, the American Tract Society, and business firms such as the Baldwin Locomotive Company, which gave 10 per cent of annual earnings during the war years. The Christian Commission waged an aggressive campaign to furnish Union soldiers with material and spiritual comforts. It sent boxes of food, clothing, and religious literature to troops and employed a large staff of delegates, mainly clergymen on leave from their congregations, to distribute supplies, preach sermons, and conduct prayer meetings in army camps and to preform such helpful services as they could for the sick and wounded.

It remained for another organization, broader in scope and more scientific in intent than any of those so far mentioned, to demonstrate the real usefulness of philanthropy in wartime. The United States Sanitary Commission, which despite its official-sounding name was privately financed and directed, was organized in June, 1861, by a group of humanitarians and reformers led by Henry W. Bellows, a Unitarian clergyman of New York City, and Dr. Elisha Harris, a well-known sanitary reformer. These men, and others like them throughout the nation, were impressed by the achievements of the British Sanitary Commission in the Crimean War and were determined to make use of the medical and sanitary knowledge acquired at such tragic cost in that conflict. Their aim, in large part realized, was to unite local relief societies into a national organization that would do much more than supplement the work of official agencies: it would use its money, influence, and knowledge to improve conditions in military camps and hospitals so as to prevent needless suffering and loss of life through disease.

In short, the tasks of the Sanitary Commission were to organize and direct the activities of thousands of women's societies and to bring the force of informed opinion to bear on the administration and military leaders. To accomplish these difficult and delicate assignments the Commission, a purely voluntary association, had to rely on persuasion and moral pressure. It would have been strange indeed if such an audacious undertaking had won universal acceptance. As it was Lincoln viewed the inception of the Commission without enthusiasm and wondered whether it might not become "a fifth wheel to the coach." The Medical Bureau, indifferent to the Commission at the start, was later often hostile. Secretary of War Stanton impeded rather than advanced its operations. And religious groups affiliated with the Christian Commission condemned the Sanitary Commission as godless. On the other hand Sanitary agents won the respect of field commanders and received enthusiastic backing from Catholics, Jews, and Protestants of liberal or advanced views. Working in or for the Sanitary Commission were veterans of prewar humanitarian crusades: Samuel Gridley Howe, for example, and able women such as Louisa Lee Schuyler, whose administrative talents later advanced many postwar reform movements. The Commission was unusually fortunate in having as its first secretary general the energetic Frederick Law Olmsted. Already famous in 1861 (and still remembered) for his books on the Old South, Olmsted brought to the Sanitary Commission the vision and foresight that he afterward applied to the planning and construction of some of America's greatest public parks.

From first to last the Sanitary Commission carried on inspections of camps and hospitals to uncover and help correct defects in sanitary arrangements, drainage, water supply, ventilation, and diet. It helped secure a needed reorganization of the Medical Bureau, promoted improvements in hospital design, and developed better and more humane methods of transporting the wounded. Through its local branches it collected food, clothing, bandages, and other supplies; stored them in supply depots; and distributed them through its agents in hospitals, on battlefields and in emergency shelters. The Commission provided lodges and feeding stations for soldiers in the major cities, established hospitals for convalescents, and maintained offices to assist distressed soldiers obtain back pay and bounties or pensions due them. It maintained a hospital directory—later adopted by the Army—which enabled relatives and other interested persons to locate the wounded and missing, collected and tabulated vital statistics on military personnel, and prepared and distributed thousands of medical monographs to surgeons in the armed forces. The greatest service rendered by the Sanitary Commission was to save lives; without it the number of deaths from disease in the Union forces—high as it was— would have been much larger. It influenced later developments in hospital administration, nursing service, and medical and surgical practice. That the Commission was a precedent for the American Red Cross goes without saying; of more immediate importance was the fact that it gave to thousands of civilians a sense of purpose and participation in the struggle for the Union.

Contributing to or raising funds for the Sanitary Commission was one practical means of obtaining that sense of participation. Numerous charitable campaigns and the Greek and Irish relief drives had already demonstrated the formidable talent of American women for fund-raising. All earlier efforts were dwarfed, however, by the giant Sanitary Fairs that the women of northern cities staged in 1863 and 1864. Through admission fees, sales or auctions of gifts, and encouragement to conspicuous giving, these carnivals of benevolence netted about half the total cash contributions to the Sanitary Commission. Fair managers received and profitably disposed of such diverse items as pianos, threshing machines, watches, jewelry, a famous trotting horse, an album containing the autographs of all the Presidents of the United States, and a cardboard representation of the American eagle "feathered" with hair cut from the heads of the President and members of the cabinet. In addition to his autograph and hair Lincoln donated a copy of his Gettysburg address and the original draft of the Emancipation Proclamation. Cornelius Vanderbilt and A. T. Stewart, determined not to be outdone by the other, each gave the New York Fair $100,000. Everywhere the fairs yielded quantities of goods of all kinds—a mixed blessing as far as the Commission was concerned, since the sudden increase in supplies created storage and transportation problems.

In spite of large sums collected at the fairs, financial questions gave the commissioners many anxious hours. Generally speaking, the branches and local societies, quick and generous in contributions of supplies, were slow and reluctant to recognize the need for money to handle and distribute supplies efficiently. The twenty-one commissioners worked without compensation except travel expenses, but the Commission at times had as many as five hundred agents, inspectors, doctors, cooks, and teamsters on its payroll. Inspections and preventive activities, which the Commission regarded as its particular contribution and which were costly to perform, lacked the emotional appeal of relief work. Other agencies competed for public sympathy and financial support, and at least two, the Christian Commission and the Western Sanitary Commission (an independent organization which conducted large-scale relief operations west of the Mississippi) were serious rivals. Bellows and Olmsted, stressing the constructive and scientific aspects of their Commission's program, looked to insurance companies for assistance; they found a valuable ally in Thomas Starr King, a popular and influential San Francisco preacher who was able to channel the lion's share of the Far West's exuberant contributions to the United States Sanitary Commission. Pope Pius IX's gift of $500 for suffering soldiers found its way, after a roundabout journey, into the treasury of the Commission. English and European branches raised some money abroad, and a rich American dentist who lived in Paris paid for the Commission's prize-winning exhibit at the Paris World's Fair of 1867. Contributions to the Sanitary Commission and its branches amounted to an estimated $25,000,000, a sum considerably larger than that raised by any of its rivals. Money gifts made up about $7,000,000 of the total, and the remainder represented the value of supplies and services furnished the Commission.

While the Sanitary and Christian Commissions organized assistance for fighting men, other groups, including many prewar abolitionists, sought means to help the Negro, for the "fundamental and astounding" result of the war, apparent long before victory had been won, was the ending of slavery. From the beginning of the war fugitive slaves had made their way to Fortress Monroe and other Union-held positions in the South, and as northern armies occupied portions of the Confederacy the number of refugee, abandoned, and captured slaves in or on Union hands rapidly increased. The status of these Negroes was at first uncertain, but step by step in 1862 actions of both the Congress and the President conferred immediate freedom on some and made it clear that emancipation awaited all. Early in 1862 societies were organized in Boston, New York, and Philadelphia to send money, clothing, books,

teachers, missionaries, and plantation supervisors to distitute
Negroes in the Sea Islands. In the next three years these
original societies swelled into regional and national freedmen's
aid associations which undertook to relieve the physical and
spiritual wants of Negroes in conquered parts of the South
and to train them for citizenship.

The relief and other assistance provided by these associations
were desperately needed. Military officers and treasury agents
had dealt with the freedmen as best they could, occasionally
in an enlightened manner. But investigations conducted in
1863 by Robert Dale Owen, Samuel Gridley Howe, and James
McKaye of the Freedmen's Inquiry Commission and James
Yeatman of the Western Sanitary Commission revealed shock-
ing conditions in the "contraband" camps and on plantations
taken over by the government and leased to private individuals.
McKaye estimated that neglect and disease had killed one-
fourth of the Negroes herded in the contraband camps. Yeatman warned that unless the conditions of the freedmen were
drastically bettered "one-half are doomed to die in the process
of freeing the rest." The freedmen's aid associations redoubled
their efforts and were able to report substantial progress in
religious uplift and education. To their credit, however, they
realized that the job was too big for private philanthropy. In
December, 1863, a joint committee representing the freedmen's
aid societies of Boston, New York, Philadelphia, and Cincinnati
urged Lincoln to recommend establishment of "a regularly
constituted government bureau, with all the machinery and
civil powers of the government behind it," to supervise and
care for freedmen. Voluntary agencies, they said, simply could
not carry out such a gigantic task "were their resources ten
times what they are, and ten times what they can be made."

It took more than a year of further agitation by the freedmen's aid societies and other interested groups before Congress, in March, 1865, authorized establishment in the War Department of a Bureau of Refugees, Freedmen, and Abandoned Land. Lincoln died before naming a commissioner for the Bureau. His successor, Andrew Johnson, acting on the advice of Secretary of War Stanton, gave the post to Major General Oliver O. Howard, a West Pointer of distinguished piety. The novelty of the federal government's assuming responsibility for the welfare and protection of large numbers of people whose rights had been little regarded either in the North or in the South assured the Bureau of a troubled existence. The act establishing the agency gave it wide but vaguely defined powers, and few of the Bureau's critics—numerous both during and after Reconstruction—charged Howard or his subordinates with failing to interpret their authority broadly or to exercise it vigorously. As a relief agency the Bureau operated on an unprecedented scale, assisting whites as well as Negroes. It leased land to freedmen, helped them find work, and supervised labor contracts with employers. It maintained courts to hear minor civil and criminal cases involving Negroes, and established hospitals, orphan homes, schools, and colleges. The relief activities of the Bureau brought the usual fears of pauperization, but Howard's policies in this sphere were prudent to the point of harshness. He decreed that help should go only to the "absolutely necessitous and destitute." In theory, at least, the Bureau attempted only to put the freedmen on the road to self-support in a free labor system.

The relation of the Freedmen's Bureau to the freedmen's aid societies (of which there were nearly thirty) provided an example, unfortunately soon forgotten, of the possibilities for fruitful co-operation between a government welfare agency and private philanthropy. The Bureau's relief activities eventually made it possible for the societies to concentrate their energies on education, the work in which they were really most interested. The Freedmen's Bureau was also interested and active in education, but such competition as developed was not between it and the private societies but between rival groups within the philanthropic ranks. Some, like the American Missionary Association, in which the Tappans were active, used education to spread religion and strengthen denominational interests. On the other hand, the Freedmen's Union Commission, a coalition of non-sectarian aid associations, stressed education pure and simple and reminded its teachers that they were not "missionaries, nor preachers, nor exhorters." The Freedmen's Bureau did not succeed in getting these rival groups to unite, and it could not ease the friction between them; but it discouraged duplication of effort in communities already supplied with schools, and it stimulated further philanthropic interests in the education of the freedmen by calling the attention of charitable organizations to those areas where need for teachers and schools was still great.

The Freedmen's Bureau did more than point out that education, prohibited under slavery, was the most urgent want of the freedmen: it provided about half the money spent on Negro education between 1865 and 1870. The Bureau leased, repaired, built, and helped build hundreds of schoolhouses. It protected schools maintained by benevolent societies, furnished transportation and quarters for teachers employed in the schools, and, although not specifically authorized to pay teachers' salaries, found means to assist the societies in meeting this expense. By the late 1860's teachers were in shorter supply than school buildings. The Bureau therefore suggested that the philanthropists establish teacher-training institutions for Negroes, and it encouraged this work by making grants to twenty normal schools, colleges, and universities. The assistance rendered by the Bureau in starting Fisk, Atlanta, and Howard Universities, as well as other institutions of higher learning for Negroes, constituted one of its most important and lasting contributions. General Howard was interested in quality as well as quantity and at one point he declined to help the American Missionary Association found more normal schools on the ground that the Association was already trying to operate more schools than it could support well.

By 1870, when the Freedmen's Bureau ceased its educational activities, the idea of Negro education had taken root in the South. The real question was not whether Negroes should be educated, but how and under whose control. Southern whites resented the Freedmen's Bureau and detested the northern teachers imported by the benevolent associations. They were not willing to allow the education of Negro children to remain permanently in the hands of persons who believed in racial equality and radical Republicanism. However, with few exceptions, such as the devoted women who spent their lives among the Negroes of the Sea Islands, Yankee teachers had gone home before the end of Reconstruction. Recognizing that the South was not yet in a position to make adequate provision for instructing any of its children, northern philanthropists such as George Peabody, John F. Slater, and Robert C. Ogden continued their efforts on behalf of Negro and southern education. But after the 1870's this assistance was accepted, and, as a matter of fact given, with the understanding that it would not violate southern institutions and traditions.

VI

"Scientific Philanthropy"

In the bestowal of charity and in prevention of
misery, the world has reached a new epoch.
DANIEL COIT GILMAN

The twenty-five or thirty years after the Civil War seemed,
to Americans living at the time, an era of stunning achievement in all fields of philanthropy. Later generations, accustomed to smile or wince at the social crudities of the Gilded
Age, have been slow to recognize that generosity and altruism
were as characteristic of the period as acquisitiveness and
self-seeking. Granted that philanthropists and those who write
about them have a tendency to dwell on what has been done
and to pass over things left undone, there was a certain foundation of fact in Robert Treat Paine's boast, made in 1893, "This
last quarter of a century has witnessed a noble outburst of
the energies of good men to help suffering brethren."
Charitable directories published in the 1880's needed as many
as a hundred pages to list and describe the numerous agencies

alleviating misery and combating disease, pauperism, ignorance, and crime. At least a part, and sometimes a generous part, of vast fortunes made by fair means or foul found its way back to the community in gifts to hospitals, libraries, art museums, churches, relief societies, orphan asylums, homes for the aged, seminaries, colleges and universities, and specialized institutions for training engineers, farmers, businessmen, physicians, dentists, pharmacists, and nurses.

When charity reformers and civic leaders of the post–Civil War generation spoke of the arrival of a new epoch in philanthropy they had something more fundamental in mind than the quantity and variety of their countrymen's giving. The magnitude and multiplicity of the outpouring for benevolent purposes rather alarmed than pleased them. What they hailed was the development of a more scientific spirit and method in philanthropy. And it was the spread of this scientific approach, bringing reforms in public welfare and private charity, that impressed them as the great humanitarian achievement of their day. At long last, or so they thought, the charitable impulse was being disciplined, the head was triumphing over the heart, the "machinery of benevolence" was coming to be understood and usefully operated, and "philanthropology," the study of the scientific principles of philanthropy, would soon be as well recognized as any other branch of learning.

The basic principles of the "new charity" would hardly have struck Joseph Tuckerman or Benjamin Franklin as novel, and the almoner who said in 1874, "I can ruin the best family in Boston by giving them a cord of food in the wrong way," spoke in the accents of Cotton Mather. The new charity was actually quite traditional in its point of view and already outdated in some of its assumptions and attributes. The scientific philanthropists of the late nineteenth century took the "do's" and "don'ts"—especially the latter—handed down from generations of charity reformers, organized them into a comprehensive system of rules, and applied them more rigorously than ever before in American history.

Although the ultimate sources of scientific philanthropy were remote, experience during and just after the Civil War provided the immediate background for its emergence. The relative success of the Sanitary and Christian Commissions gave new prestige to voluntary action. The Sanitary Commission, in particular, with its emphasis on visitation, inspection, and advisory functions, influenced the development of both official and voluntary agencies in the postwar years. The public health movement benefited from the wartime interest in camp and hospital improvement. A committee of sanitarians, which likened the poor population of New York City to "an immense army in camp, upon small territory, crowded into old filthy dwellings, and without the slightest police regulations for cleanliness," secured a reorganization of health services in the metropolis which was ultimately copied in other cities. Similarly, the belief that veterans were involved in the wave of crime and disorders that followed the war revived enthusiasm for prison reform and stimulated fresh interest in all branches of social science. War commissions and relief associations gave countless men and women of philanthropic disposition a taste for service and an experience in authority they were reluctant to surrender after hostilities were over.

One of those who was not ready to quit was Reverend Henry W. Bellows of the now defunct Sanitary Commission. Another was Miss Clara Barton, who had conducted her battlefield relief operations independent of the Sanitary Commission or any other authority. In 1866 Bellows and some of the men who had worked with him in the Sanitary Commission organized the American Association for the Relief of Misery on the Battlefield. For five years they sought unsuccessfully to obtain American ratification of the Geneva Convention of 1864 providing for neutralization of aid to the wounded in time of war. The connection between the Sanitary Commission, the Association for the Relief of Misery on the Battlefield, and the Red Cross movement is plain, but it was Miss Barton, not the Bellows group, who eventually established the American Red Cross and secured the adherence of the United States to the Geneva treaty.

Clara Barton was a unique character in her own or any generation. Had she chosen to do so she might have qualified for Dorothea Dix's corps of Civil War nurses, for she met the standards of maturity and plainness. She was born in North Oxford, Massachusetts, on Christmas Day, 1821, and once said of herself, "I was never what the world would call 'even good looking.'" Yet she was, by her own account, and despite a stature of little more than five feet, an "imposing figure." She had a magnetism that commanded loyalty and an imperiousness that led one of her close and devoted associates to call her "the Queen." Miss Barton had a remarkable talent for dramatizing herself. "I wrung the blood from the bottom of my clothing before I could step, for the weight about my feet," she wrote in one of her Civil War letters. She took herself and her work very seriously. These are useful qualities for leadership in any public enterprise—and Clara Barton had in addition the *sine qua non* of all the great humanitarians: "What is nobody's business is my business," she said, and believed.

"Scientific Philanthropy"

After the Civil War Miss Barton occupied herself for several years in lecturing on her battlefield activities, in checking hospital and burial records to obtain information for answering inquiries from relatives of missing prisoners of war, and in identifying and marking the graves of thousands of soldiers. She happened to be in Switzerland in 1870 and there met officials of the International Committee of the Red Cross. Work with the German Red Cross in the Franco-Prussian War brought her new laurels and popular identification with the Red Cross movement. In 1877 the Russo-Turkish War summoned her out of semiretirement and fired her ambition to found an American Red Cross society that would centralize and systematize relief activities in such emergencies. It was an uphill struggle, but in 1881 she incorporated the American Association of the Red Cross, and in the following year she had the immense satisfaction of seeing the long-delayed American ratification of the Geneva Convention become a reality.

Clara Barton's success in these campaigns stemmed in part from her ability to explain the provision of the Geneva treaty and the functions of the International Committee of the Red Cross in such a way as to allay American suspicions of foreign involvements even in humanitarian undertakings. But more important, both in the short and the long run, was her conception of the American Red Cross as an agency for rendering assistance in times of peace as well as war. In her propaganda as well as in the constitution of the new society she emphasized opportunities and responsibilities for service in plague, fire, flood, drought, and accident. As the historian of the American Red Cross has pointed out, her idea of what the Red Cross could and should do in peacetime made sense to people who saw no danger of war but who had recently raised large funds for victims of the Chicago and Boston fires and who were all too familiar with the havoc wrought by natural disasters, epidemics, and appalling railway and mine accidents. For most of the twenty-five years that Miss Barton dominated the American Red Cross, disaster relief was the organization's major activity. Although sixty years old in 1881 when her service with the Red Cross began, she administered relief in person and on the spot both in domestic catastrophes such as the Johnstown flood of 1889 and the Sea Island hurricane of 1893, and in foreign crises such as the Armenian massacres of 1896.

The peculiar nature of disaster relief, not to mention Miss Barton's vigorous personality and individualistic methods of operation, put the American Red Cross, in its formative years, outside the mainstream of late nineteenth-century philanthropy. To say this implies no discredit to Miss Barton or to the organization she founded. The Red Cross, which in practice meant Clara Barton, was not engaged in charity as the word is usually interpreted. Miss Barton had a sensible aversion to pauperizing recipients of Red Cross aid, but she was not as hagridden by the fear of pauperism as so many of her contemporaries were. She wanted to give temporary help to normal people who were victims of abnormal misfortune and to render such assistance as she could to restore them to their normal way of life. That, it must be said, was all that those she aided seem to have wanted or expected. As Miss Barton's critics within the Red Cross were to point out, she had no taste and small talent for organizational or administrative refinements. But surely her singular and endearing characteristic was lack of interest in reforming anything or anybody. She did not launch crusades to end wars, famines, plagues, fires, or floods; she simply met emergencies as they arose and to the

best of her abilities. Thus, although the comparison is somewhat strained, she belongs in the tradition of Stephen Girard
rather than of Benjamin Rush.

Miss Barton once served briefly as superintendent of a
women's reformatory in Massachusetts, but her Red Cross
work hardly touched the problem of greatest concern to advocates of scientific philanthropy. This was the treatment of
people who, even in normal times, were dependent on public
or private bounty for all or part of their support. Massachusetts,
the pioneer in so much nineteenth-century social legislation,
took a step toward more intelligent handling of the problem in
1863 by creating a Board of State Charities. In the next decade
ten other states followed Massachusetts' example. As a general
rule the members of these state boards had no administrative
responsibilities; they served without pay (in order to make the
offices unattractive to spoilsmen); and their duties were to
inspect, report upon, and make recommendations for improving public welfare institutions and such private ones as received
state assistance. In an era not notable for the excellence of its
public servants, the members and secretaries of these boards
—Samuel G. Howe, Franklin B. Sanborn, Josephine Shaw
Lowell, and Frederick H. Wines, to mention but a few of
a distinguished company—set high standards of integrity and
competence.

The task of bringing greater efficiency and more humanity
into state welfare services required persistent effort. In New
York and New Jersey the state boards of charity received
strong backing from State Charities Aid Associations, voluntary
organizations whose membership and program had some resemblance to the wartime auxiliaries of the Sanitary Commission. The National Conference of Charities and Correction,

a creation of the state boards, grew into a late-nineteenth-century version of the Benevolent Empire of the 1830's and became one of the most powerful agencies for spreading the doctrines of scientific philanthropy. Even so, progress was slow. The boards and their allies represented informed opinion, but legislatures were not bound to follow their recommendations, and they exercised only shadowy supervision over local poor-relief officers. Nevertheless the boards began the work of policing almshouses, insane asylums, orphanages, and schools for the blind and deaf. They resumed the struggle to obtain state care for the pauper insane and secured establishment of new asylums, training schools, and reformatories. They worked diligently to get dependent children out of almshouses and into state schools, county or private orphanages, or foster homes.

The care of the dependent classes, burdensome enough in normal times, became an even more serious problem when periods of depression vastly increased the number of people needing and demanding assistance. The hardship and destitution caused by the depression of 1873–78 were like the effects of a nationwide natural disaster. Private citizens, the older charitable organizations, and public authorities responded by setting up soup kitchens, breadlines, and free lodging houses, and by distributing coal and food to the poor in their homes. In the emergency little attention was paid to investigation of need, tests of destitution, or safeguards against the possibility that some of the needy might be receiving help from several sources at the same time. First come, first served, was the rule.

Persons of substantial means and enlightened opinion who worried in normal times about the financial cost and social consequences of improper care of the dependent classes were horrified by the excess of "kindly but mistaken charities" during the depression. They deplored the "profuse and chaotic" distribution of private charitable assistance to the "clamorous and impudent," and they complained that much of the municipal expenditures for poor relief went to impostors or grafting politicians and that such doles as did reach the needy had a bad effect on their character and willingness to work. This "peevish fault finding," as contemporary critics called it, was little appreciated in the early stages of the depression. "Are we to let people starve because the means of relief which are attainable are such that we may not regard as altogether the best possible?" asked the New York *Daily Graphic* in 1874. When charity reformers criticized James Gordon Bennett's gift of $30,000 to a soup kitchen, the *Graphic* pointed out that Bennett's scheme gave "all soup and no salary," whereas professional philanthropy proposed "all salary and no soup."

It was not salaries that the so-called professional philanthropists demanded (although paid charity agents began to be employed during the depression) but something better than soup and alms for the poor. They wanted better organization of relief operations, more discrimination in the bestowal of assistance, and more attention to the individual needs of the persons helped. Much of their emphasis, it must be admitted, was negative. They did not urge improved administration of public relief but cessation of all public aid to the poor outside of institutions. Outdoor relief, defined by one of its opponents as "the paying out of funds raised by taxation from provident men to support the improvident in their homes" had long been in ill repute, and toward the end of the depression taxpayers in Brooklyn and Philadelphia were sufficiently aroused and well organized to put an end to it. The saving of money effected by this action in the two cities, and the beneficent results it was thought to have in compelling would-be paupers to become self-supporting, confirmed charity reformers in the belief that outdoor relief was both undesirable and unnecessary. Private charity, properly organized and administered, could do all that needed to be done for the poor who did not require institutional care.

First, however, private charity must be purged of its sentimentality and organized into an effective force. Jewish welfare agencies had joined in Philadelphia in 1870 and in New York in 1874 to form the United Hebrew Charities, and during the depression charitable societies in the larger cities made some efforts to co-operate in detecting impostors and rounders. But it was the example of the London Charity Organization Society, founded in 1869, which most impressed those Americans who were seeking (as a Philadelphia group said) "a method by which idleness and begging, now so encouraged, may be suppressed and worthy self-respecting poverty be discovered and relieved at the smallest cost to the benevolent." Societies patterned after the London C.O.S. began to be organized in the United States in the late 1870's and multiplied rapidly in the 1880's. For the rest of the century, "charity organization" and "scientific philanthropy" were virtually synonymous.

Charity organization meant just that. As originally conceived it emphatically did not mean the granting of relief by the charity organization societies. The founders of these societies believed that there were already too many agencies engaged in giving alms and old clothes to the poor. "No RELIEF GIVEN HERE," announced signs at the entrance to the Buffalo C.O.S., and Josephine Shaw Lowell of the New York C.O.S. did not hesitate to advise prospective donors that all the organization's funds went for administrative expenses and not one cent to the poor.

The basic idea of the charity organization movement was to promote co-operation and higher standards of efficiency among the older relief-dispensing agencies. This objective was regarded as presumptuous by some firmly intrenched agencies who were well satisfied with their own methods and jealous of their prerogatives. With varying degrees of success, therefore, the charity organization societies acted as clearinghouses and bureaus of information. They maintained registries of all applicants for relief, with detailed records of the assistance given or refused by co-operating societies, and they undertook searching investigation of the need and worthiness of the "cases" referred to them. When they discovered a "helpable" applicant, they attempted to find employment for him, or referred him to the relief-dispensing agency best suited to meet his particular need. Through force of circumstances, and not without qualms of conscience, some of the charity organization societies actually became purveyors of relief. Usually, however, they preferred to help the poor by providing such services as penny savings banks, coal-saving funds, provident wood-yards, day nurseries for the children of working mothers, and workrooms where women could be trained to become nursemaids, laundresses, or seamstresses.

In theory, "friendly visiting" of the poor in their homes by volunteers working under the supervision of paid agents was the core—or better, the heart—of charity organization. By this means ties of sympathy and personal interest were to be established between the rich and the poor, and the poor were to be permanently improved and uplifted. The visitors were

not to be almoners, for almsgiving was counterfeit philanthropy. Instead of stray coins, visitors were to bring encouragement and advice to the people they visited. From the
writings of Octavia Hill, an English philanthropic worker,
American C.O.S. leaders culled the following suggestions for
volunteer visitors:

> You want to know them,—to enter into their lives, their thoughts;
> to let them enter into some of your brightness; to make their lives
> a little fuller, a little gladder. You who know so much more than
> they, might help them so much at important crises of their lives.
> You might gladden their homes by bringing them flowers, or, bet-
> ter still, by teaching them to grow plants; you might meet them
> face to face as friends; you might teach them; you might collect
> their savings; you might sing for and with them; you might take
> them into the parks or out for quiet days in the country, in small
> companies, or to your own or your friends' grounds, or to exhibi-
> tions or picture galleries; you might teach and refine and make them
> cleaner by merely going among them.

Miss Hill conceded that the poor, in their turn, might teach
the visitors patience, vigor, and content. But in general hardly
anyone active in the movement at the start questioned that the
visitors were morally as well as materially superior to the
visited.

This conviction of superiority, like most of the original
charity organization program, rested on certain assumptions
about the causes of poverty and dependency. As a rule the
charity reformers were so preoccupied with pauperism that
they gave little serious thought to poverty. To the extent that
they did think about poverty they accepted the view that it
was caused by weaknesses of character, body, or intellect, and
curable by reform of the individual. Josephine Shaw Lowell
(1843–1905), the principal founder of the New York C.O.S.,

is a case in point. As she saw it, building character rather than relieving need was the true aim of the society's work. It is not "the poor" but "our brothers" who are our concern, she said. She took it for granted that those brothers were a young and untutored lot who needed stern discipline and careful training.

Mrs. Lowell was a woman of the leisure class who devoted forty years of her life to public service. But to say this does scant justice to the force of character and sturdy good sense that won the respect of her contemporaries. Born into a family of wealth, culture, and liberal leanings, she was the sister of one war hero and the wife of another. All the circumstances of her life, from fortunate birth to tragic widowhood, thrust her into a career of service. She brought to her work self-discipline, matter-of-factness, and a kindness which, if not indulgent, was all embracing. Kindness in her case was based not on sentimentality but on a religious conviction that each human being deserved good from every other because all were sons of God and had an eternal future. Mrs. Lowell was made of sterner stuff than some philanthropists. Although she wrote often of the duty of charity, she did not make a point of stressing, as Cotton Mather, Amos Lawrence, and many others had, the pleasures and privileges of giving.

As Mrs. Lowell saw it, the world was made up of two classes: workers and idlers. Workers might do or be many things, provided their activities were useful; idlers, in her succinct definition, were people who lived off the workers. Unfortunately, workers had a natural inclination to become idlers. The mass of men and women, Mrs. Lowell maintained, needed the pressure of necessity to force them to exercise their faculties. Hence it was dangerous to do too much for anyone lest he lose the ability and appetite for work. Like other charity reformers of her generation Mrs. Lowell also believed that certain undesirable social traits were transmitted from generation to generation and that some groups had a hereditary tendency toward pauperism and crime. Neither Mrs. Lowell nor her co-workers accepted the conclusion of the extreme Social Darwinists that all acts of mercy to the weak in body and mind tended to degrade the human race, but they did advocate putting chronic paupers into strictly supervised institutions so that the vicious and degraded would not perpetuate their kind.

It is not surprising that Mrs. Lowell and other founders of the charity organization movement should have been influenced by the notions of political economy and natural science current in the 1870's and 80's. More significant is the fact that those ideas seem to have had little effect on the actual working of the societies. Charity organization best demonstrated its claim to be scientific by allowing the demands of reality to override the hypotheses with which it began. Investigations, originally undertaken as a species of detective work to discover fraud came to be regarded as diagnoses to ascertain facts needed to treat distress intelligently. Salaried workers, although outnumbered by volunteer friendly visitors, played an increasingly important part in the work of the societies. These paid workers, who supervised and trained the volunteers, were already numerous enough in the 1890's to suggest that a new profession was in the making. In practice, charity organization societies became centers to which people in trouble applied for help in locating agencies that could assist them. Odd and indirect as this service sounds, it was a useful one in large cities where the very abundance of specialized benevolent associations made for confusion. The societies never gave up their efforts to improve and co-ordinate charitable work, and they proved their value in the depression of 1893–97, when new societies were founded, faltering ones revived, and flourishing ones took on new vigor.

Because scientific philanthropy insisted on gathering the facts about the specific causes of each applicant's need, C.O.S. case workers had to report and deal with poverty-producing factors that had little to do with the sufferers' characters. The caseworkers attributed as many as possible of these situations to moral lapses, but even before the gray nineties they were well aware of environmental causes of distress. The labor disputes of the eighties and nineties made some leaders of the "new charity" wonder whether the newest might not be justice in work and wages. Mrs. Lowell resigned from the New York State Board of Charity in 1889 because she felt that the interests of the working people were of paramount importance. "It is better to save them before they go under, than to spend your life fishing them out when they're half drowned and taking care of them afterwards!" she said. "I must try to help them, if I can, and leave the broken down paupers to others."

For at least three-quarters of a century charity reformers had been seeking to prevent pauperism. They had often expressed the opinion that the first duty of the community was not to feed the hungry and clothe the naked but to prevent people from becoming hungry and naked. By 1893 Robert Treat Paine, president of the Associated Charities of Boston since its founding, was of the opinion that the social order itself needed housecleaning. "Pauperism cannot be wisely considered alone," he said, "but the problem of how to uplift the general level of life must be studied as *one whole problem*." The remedies proposed were still less fundamental than the language of those who advanced them suggested. Scientific philanthropy and social reform had not yet quite joined forces but they were drawing closer together.

VII

Benevolent Trusts and Distrusts

If a combination to do business is effective in saving waste and in getting better results, why is not combination far more important in philanthropic work?

JOHN D. ROCKEFELLER

The most famous document in the history of American philanthropy—although the word philanthropy does not appear in it—is an article entitled "Wealth" published in the *North American Review* in June, 1889. The author was the "Star-Spangled Scotchman," Andrew Carnegie. Born in a weaver's cottage in Dunfermline, Scotland, in 1835, Carnegie had come to the United States in 1848. As the eldest son of a poor family, he was old if not large for his years, and at the age of twelve cheerfully and self-confidently assumed the responsibilities of breadwinner. "Anybody can get along in this Country" he wrote in 1852. "If I don't it will be my own fault." Andrew Carnegie, likable, alert, shrewd, and able got along famously. By 1889, thirty times a millionaire, he had been a rich man

for more than twenty years. For him the question had long been not how to gain wealth but what to do with it. He had reached some conclusions on the problem as early as 1868 and in 1887 had told his friend William E. Gladstone that he considered it a disgrace to die rich. Now, in his famous essay, he proposed that millionaires, instead of bequeathing vast fortunes to heirs or making benevolent grants by will, should administer their wealth as a public trust during life.

The year of Carnegie's birth was also the year in which Tocqueville published *Democracy in America*. Of all the changes that had swept over American society in the fifty-odd years since 1835, one of the most striking was the arrival of that race of rich men whose absence Tocqueville had noted. Carnegie certainly did not doubt that there was a "millionaire class" in the United States. It was to this class that he addressed himself. In assumption of superiority Carnegie went far beyond the charity reformers. His view resembled that of John Winthrop and William Penn, except in one important respect. Carnegie did not say, as those men had, that the great ones owed their distinction to peculiar arrangements ordained of God. He attributed the eminence of the millionaire class to fitness to survive and triumph in the competitive struggle. The trusteeship Carnegie proposed thus differed from traditional doctrines of stewardship. The millionaire, a product of natural selection, was an agent of the public, of the forces of civilization, rather than a servant of God. Trusteeship devolved on the man of wealth because he was fittest to exercise it. In the exercise of his trust he was responsible only to his own conscience and judgment of what was best for the community.

An English critic, astounded by the brashness of Carnegie's scheme, named it the gospel of wealth to distinguish it from the gospel of Christianity. With customary good humor Carnegie accepted the label, and, as usual, he won the encounter; for who can deny that "the gospel of wealth" sounds better and stronger than "wealth"? As a matter of fact there were religious overtones in Carnegie's gospel. He was willing to have the scriptural passage about the difficulty of rich men entering the kingdom of Heaven interpreted strictly, and he believed that laboring for the good of one's fellows was the essence of Christ's teaching. But, as Carnegie frankly admitted, he did not believe that under modern conditions much good could be accomplished by imitating the life or methods of Christ. Let the laws of accumulation and distribution be left free; let the able and energetic dispose of their surplus as they saw fit; the millionaire class, working toward the same objectives as Christ, but (as Carnegie said) "laboring in a different manner," would someday bring "Peace on earth, among men good will."

According to the gospel of wealth, philanthropy was less the handmaid of social reform than a substitute for it. Wise administration of wealth was an antidote for radical proposals for redistributing property and a method of reconciling the poor and the rich. Carnegie spoke of "the temporary unequal distribution of wealth"; however, like his mentor, Herbert Spencer, he thought that it would take eons, an overturn of natural laws of economics, and an almost inconceivable revolution in human nature to erase that inequality. He believed it was a waste of time to challenge evolutionary processes, and he was firmly convinced that the only alternative to the system that rewarded millionaires with palaces and laborers with cottages was one that would condemn all to hovels. But Carnegie was no less convinced that "administrators of surplus wealth"—his term for philanthropists—had it in their power to bestow benefactions of lasting benefit on their weaker and poorer brethren.

Had Carnegie chosen to do so, he might have said simply that men possessed of more wealth than they could possibly use would be well advised to employ it for the public good. Possibly that was all he really meant. The arrogance of his language and the despotic tendencies of his philosophy should not blind us to the fact that his solution for the problem of surplus wealth was neither entirely new nor inconsistent with American traditions. Although Carnegie preached and practiced giving on an undreamed-of scale he did not propose that philanthropy should shoulder the whole burden of welfare. Far from it. Recognizing the responsibility of the state to care for the destitute and helpless, he urged the millionaire class to concentrate its philanthropic efforts on the able and industrious. His advice suited the temper of the times and the inclinations of self-made men. Coming after so many years of emphasis on the cause and cure of pauperism it infused new vigor into philanthropy.

Carnegie was as contemptuous of almsgiving and as fearful of impulsive generosity as the most doctrinaire charity reformer. "To assist, but rarely or never to do all," was the rule he laid down. Although he made a few bows in the direction of reforming the character and improving the morals of the poor, the assistance which had seemed most valuable to many nineteenth-century philanthropists, he was not really interested in those who needed this kind of help. The uplift he favored was of a different and less direct variety: libraries, parks, concert halls, museums, "swimming baths," and institutions such as Cooper Union and Pratt Institute, both of

Clara Barton. (From Clara Barton, *The Red Cross*, Washington, D.C.: American National Red Cross, 1898.)

Dorothea Dix. (From a portrait in the New Jersey State Hospital, Trenton; reproduced by permission.)

Andrew Carnegie. (From *Life Magazine*, April 13, 1905.)

which he greatly admired. Significantly he called these agencies "ladders upon which the aspiring can rise."

At the start of the 1890's the New York *Tribune* figured the number of persons in the millionaire class at 4,047. Few of these men and women seem to have taken literally Carnegie's assertion that it was a disgrace to die rich. Some of them, however, already were and long had been distributing a part of their surplus during life. Just how many were so disposed and exactly how much they gave it is not now possible to say. An investigation of their giving habits made by the *Review of Reviews* in 1893 reached the sensible albeit equivocal conclusion that cities would be poorer without the parks, museums, libraries, and technical institutes provided by generous millionaires, and considerably richer if more men and women of wealth followed the example of those who gave. This interesting, although not necessarily reliable, survey indicated that the percentage of millionaires who "recognized their obligations" varied from city to city. Baltimore, with 49 per cent of her millionaires listed as active givers, ranked highest on the list and New York, where millionaires were most numerous but apparently least generous, was at the bottom. Donors in different cities had distinct preferences: Cincinnati's millionaires supported musical and artistic ventures; those in Minneapolis gave to the state university and the public library; and Philadelphians were interested in overseas relief, Arctic exploration, and the education of Indians and Negroes. Boston, surprisingly, made a poor showing. "Our Boston millionaires," reported the local investigator, "give money when it is solicited (properly), and they all include in their wills some bequests to Harvard and to Massachusetts General Hospital. That is all."

Of all the ladders for those who aspired, free libraries and educational institutions with a practical slant struck capitalists of the 1880's and 90's as most inspiring. Carnegie's own benefactions, like those of so many philanthropists, began with the donation of a library to his home town, and he ultimately gave a library building to almost every community which provided a site and promised to maintain the building. He regarded Enoch Pratt, donor of the Pratt Free Library in Baltimore as "the ideal disciple of the gospel of wealth." Carnegie and other businessmen gave generously to Negro industrial schools, such as Hampton and Tuskegee, which elevated manual and domestic training into character-building disciplines. They were much less generous toward Negro institutions of higher learning. Only a trickle of philanthropic aid, mainly furnished by church groups, went to these struggling, poorly housed and equipped colleges, but, meager as it was, this assistance helped keep them alive. Students at Fisk University took financing into their own hands. Through concert tours in Europe and America the Fisk Jubilee Singers raised funds which permitted the institution to move from dilapidated army barracks to a new building appropriately named Jubilee Hall.

Although some business leaders thought higher education almost as detrimental to whites as to Negroes, colleges and universities continued to be beneficiaries of the millionaires' surplus wealth. "Here is a noble use of wealth," Carnegie said of Leland Stanford's audacious plan to build a university in the Far West, a project which in 1889 was believed to involve the greatest sum ever given by an individual for any purpose. Stanford's avowed purpose was to create a new kind of university which would give a practical rather than a theoretical education. Albert Shaw observed admiringly that the donor was going about the task in the same businesslike fashion he had employed in building the great stock farm where his fast horses were bred.

John D. Rockefeller (1839–1937) was an old hand at giving when, in May, 1889, a month before the appearance of Carnegie's "Wealth," he made an initial contribution of $600,000 toward founding the new University of Chicago. He was then approaching fifty and had been rich, and getting richer, for twenty-five years. But Rockefeller did not wait until he had a surplus before beginning to give. His account book for 1855, the year he went to work, recorded small but frequent contributions to charity, Sunday school, and missions. In the 1850's the amounts sometimes totaled a tenth of his income, and they increased over the years. Even so Rockefeller's benefactions were hard pressed to keep up with his accumulations. Thus in 1888, when he donated $170,000 to various good works, dividends from the Standard Oil combination were returning millions. Not even the rising University of Chicago, to which he gave $1 million in 1890 and a like sum in 1892, the latter "as a special thank-offering to Almighty God for returning health," could drain off his surplus.

The responsibility of wealth pressed as heavily on Rockefeller as on Carnegie. If possible, Rockefeller felt the burden even more than Carnegie, since he adhered to the old-fashioned religious doctrine of stewardship rather than to the new gospel of wealth. Amos Lawrence might have said, as Rockefeller did, "The good Lord gave me the money," but Carnegie certainly did not. As archaic as the sentiment sounds, there is no reason to doubt that Rockefeller sincerely believed it. He thought that the good Lord had given him the money for a purpose and expected him to handle it with care. The steward was faithful to his trust. Rockefeller was quite willing to give, but he felt an obligation to inquire into the worthiness of the causes to which he was asked to contribute. By 1891 he complained that these investigations were taking as much of his time and energy as the affairs of Standard Oil. Help came in the person of a thirty-eight-year-old Baptist clergyman, Frederick T. Gates, who agreed to assist Rockefeller in his benefactions by interviewing supplicants, making inquiries, and suggesting action. As a former fund-raiser Gates was wise in the ways of money-seekers. In his charge, as Gates himself recalled, Rockefeller soon found himself "laying aside retail giving almost wholly, and entering safely and pleasurably into the field of wholesale philanthropy."

Rockefeller's entry into the field of wholesale philanthropy set off a controversy—mainly one-sided, since Rockefeller did not reply to the attack—that continued for at least a quarter of a century. In 1895 Washington Gladden, minister of the First Congregational Church in Columbus, Ohio, and a leader of the social gospel movement, published an article, "Tainted Money," in which he outdid Emerson and antedated Thorstein Veblen in denouncing the ways of trade. Although Gladden did not mention any multimillionaire by name, his attack on the benefactions of "robber barons," "Roman plunderers," "pirates of industry," and "spoilers of the state" was thought to be directed at the Rockefeller philanthropies. Gladden had stated in a sermon delivered to the National Conference of Charities and Corrections in 1893 that the central consideration of charity should be the effect of the gift upon the character of the recipient. Now he raised the question whether a church or university could take offerings of money made in morally reprehensible ways without condoning the methods and accepting the standards of the donor. "Is this clean money?" he asked. "Can any man, can any institution, knowing its origin, touch it without being defiled?"

This was a hard question and it was taken seriously in the 1890's and 1900's when nearly every issue seemed at bottom a moral one. It came up again in 1905 when Gladden and other liberal clergymen objected to the acceptance by the Congregational Board of Foreign Missions of a $100,000 gift from Rockefeller. The controversy simmered down after it was revealed that the Board had solicited Rockefeller for the money. Moral questions are notoriously difficult to resolve and in this case no consensus could be reached because Rockefeller's character was defended as ardently as it was attacked, and eminent moralists pointed out that the purpose of the gift was as worthy of consideration, and easier to judge, than the origin of the money.

Jane Addams (1860–1935) of Hull House, who was already beginning to occupy an unenviable distinction as "the conscience of the nation," was one of the few public figures who viewed the tainted money issue with detachment. In the 1890's she rejected an offer of $20,000 for a Hull House project on the grounds that the donor's bad record as an employer made it unthinkable to accept his sponsorship of the undertaking, a co-operative boarding house for working girls, but she refused to become embroiled in the public debate over tainted money. Her conscience was sensitive and she was accustomed to drawing fine ethical distinctions. As a rule, however, she avoided passing moral judgments on people. It was the unrighteousness of conditions that troubled her, and movements for the fulfilment of democracy that excited her.

Miss Addams had founded Hull House, the best known of

the early settlement houses, in the same year—1889—that Andrew Carnegie enunciated the gospel of wealth. Like him, she hoped to establish ties of sympathy between rich and poor, but her purpose and methods differed from his. She made those differences clear when she confessed that the settlement movement was based on emotion as much as conviction, that it represented an outlet for sentiments of universal brotherhood, and that it appealed to persons who had "a bent to express in social service and in terms of action the spirit of Christ." While Carnegie proposed building ladders upon which the ambitious poor could rise, Miss Addams and other settlement leaders went to live with the poor. The settlement houses were designed to offer educated young men and women a means of getting in touch with the "starvation struggle" of the masses. Once the settlement workers had established friendly relations with their underprivileged neighbors and learned their needs, they could join with them in efforts to improve the common life. Perhaps this was a species of uplift. Jane Addams called it "the arousing of social energies."

Settlement houses were only one manifestation of the current of religious humanitarianism stirring in churches and among individuals of all faiths. Around the turn of the century other forces and a host of voluntary associations were at work or organizing to strengthen the social framework of democracy and to restore and extend the principles of self-government. But settlement residents, as Miss Addams pointed out as early as 1892, were "bound to see the needs of their neighborhoods as a whole, to furnish data for legislation, and to use their influence to secure it." Uncommitted to any particular program except flexibility and experimentation, the settlements contributed to nearly all the social movements of the early twentieth century. Settlement leaders including Miss Addams, Lillian Wald, Mary McDowell, Eleanor McMain, Mary Kingsbury Simkhovitch, and others of equal prominence, were formidable champions of the interests of women, children, and immigrants, and effective campaigners for improved housing, health, and recreation. The common attribute of these women was ability to reduce abstract issues to human terms and to translate high ideals into prosaic practice. In working with and for their neighborhoods they came to realize that "prevention," so long the watchword of the reformer, was not enough. There were unsatisfied needs in every community, whether for playgrounds, nurseries, or some closer approximation of social justice, which could be met only by positive action.

It was a sign of new ways of thought that after the 1890's the term "social work" began to replace "scientific philanthropy." The change was related to the growing number of paid workers in welfare agencies and to the development of training courses in applied philanthropy which, by 1910, had become schools of social work. Meanwhile new leaders such as Mary Richmond (1861–1928) and Edward T. Devine (1867–1948) had assumed direction of the charity organization movement. Miss Richmond, who occupied important positions in the Baltimore and Philadelphia charity organization societies and the Russell Sage Foundation, strove to put casework on a professional basis. Through her book *Social Diagnosis* (1917), she exercised a dominant influence on both the philosophy and methods of social work. Devine, as secretary of the New York C.O.S. and editor of the influential social work magazine, *The Survey*, brought the new profession into the forefront of the social reform movements of the Progressive era. In the 1900's social workers retained the old dislike of relief and cautious attitude toward charity. But where scientific philanthropists of an earlier generation had deplored charity seekers, social workers criticized the conditions that made charity necessary. Poverty rather than pauperism was now the bugaboo, improvement of the general standard of living the remedy.

Inspired by new hopes and visions, but still struggling with the old problem of misery, social workers sometimes expressed misgivings about the nature and tendencies of philanthropy. Was the benefactor-beneficiary relationship a denial of the equality democracy implied? Did charity perpetuate the conditions that created poverty? Could philanthropy, tied as it was to the purse strings of the classes who benefited most from the existing order, accomplish anything of importance in building a better society? The same or similar questions were being raised by critics outside of social work, although not so much in inquiry as in condemnation. To practicing philanthropists who were also democrats and social reformers these were matters of grave import. If answers were not immediately forthcoming, the very fact that the questions were raised and thoughtfully considered had a wholesome influence on philanthropic developments.

Developments of great significance were under way. Rockefeller and Carnegie had retired from business in 1897 and 1901, respectively, but they still faced the problem of what to do with mounting fortunes. By 1901 even wholesale philanthropy of the sort each had been practicing for a decade was inadequate to dispose of accumulations totaling not tens but hundreds of millions. Some more effective method of organizing and conducting what Rockefeller called "this business of benevolence" must be devised. To Rockefeller the answer was plain. Put your surplus money in a trust, he advised the "men of worth and position" gathered to celebrate the tenth anniversary of the founding of the University of Chicago: "Let us erect a foundation, a trust, and engage directors who will make it a life work to manage, with our personal co-operation, this business of benevolence properly and effectively."

In the dozen years after 1901, as if to prove that philanthropy could be made a successful venture, Rockefeller, Carnegie, and other donors established a series of foundations that made earlier philanthropic ventures seem somewhat amateurish. The Rockefeller Institute for Medical Research (1901), General Education Board (1902), Carnegie Foundation for the Advancement of Teaching (1905), Milbank Memorial Fund (1905), Russell Sage Foundation (1907), Carnegie Corporation of New York (1911), and Rockefeller Foundation (1913) do not exhaust the list of foundations organized during the period, but their number, and even the size of their capital assets, was less significant than the boldness of the enterprise to which they were committed. Most earlier charitable trusts had been established for some narrowly defined purpose. The smaller Carnegie funds, designed to promote the donor's particular philanthropic interests, continued in this tradition. The major trusts founded by Carnegie and Rockefeller, however, were limited only to the advancement of knowledge and human welfare. Relieving the needy was not their objective. They would attack misery at its source through the weapon of research.

The advent of the foundations coincided with the era of muckraking and trustbusting, with a leftward trend in politics, growing militancy in the ranks of labor, and a general fear of bigness. According to popular legend John D. Rockefeller, alarmed by muckracking attacks such as Ida M. Tarbell's

History of the Standard Oil Company (1904), employed a public relations counselor, Ivy Lee, who advised him to increase his benefactions in order to buy public favor. Actually Lee did not become associated with Rockefeller until 1914, more than twenty years after Rockefeller had become a wholesale philanthropist. Frederick T. Gates, the principal architect of Rockefeller's benefactions, was aware of and presumably not averse to allaying popular animosity toward his employer. Gates, however, was a clergyman and businessman rather than a public relations expert. He was mainly concerned with helping Rockefeller administer a vast fortune wisely and beneficently.

Interestingly enough, the organization of large philanthropic trusts aroused little opposition until 1910. In that year a bill to incorporate the Rockefeller Foundation was introduced in Congress. By this time anything bearing Rockefeller's name or financed by Standard Oil money was bound to provoke controversy. Opponents revived the slogans of the tainted-money debate and likened Rockefeller's gifts to the Trojan horse and the kiss of Judas. The move was all the more resented because the federal government was prosecuting the Standard Oil combination for violation of the Sherman Antitrust Act. In 1911 the Supreme Court ordered dissolution of Standard Oil of New Jersey, the center of the Rockefeller empire. The decision made it unlikely that Congress would charter a new Rockefeller trust, even a benevolent one. The opposition of the Taft administration further weakened the foundation bill's chances for passage. Attorney General George Wickersham called the measure "an indefinite scheme for perpetuating vast wealth." President William Howard Taft also expressed disapproval of "the proposed act to incorporate John D. Rockefeller." In 1913, rebuffed by the federal government, Rockefeller incorporated the foundation under the laws of New York State.

The next two years were difficult ones for the foundations. In 1914 several members of the United States Senate attempted to prohibit the Department of Agriculture from accepting grants provided by the General Education Board for farm demonstration work in the South. Meanwhile, the United States Industrial Relations Commission, a body established by Congress to study the underlying causes of industrial unrest, broadened its investigation to include the operation of philanthropic foundations. The newly organized Rockefeller Foundation was a particular target of attack, but in 1915 the Commission's director of research arraigned all foundations for their wealth, loosely defined powers, exemption from federal taxation, freedom from public control, subserviency to donors, and benumbing effect on smaller philanthropic agencies and individual giving. None of this criticism led to legislative action against the foundations. But since the attitudes of beneficiaries are as important in philanthropy as the desires and purposes of benefactors, it is significant that the early foundations began their work in a somewhat hostile atmosphere.

The fear, however, was mainly of possible abuse of power in the future. Even as this suspicion was expressed, other voices were calling attention to the present need for the foundations and to their possibilities for good. The Russell Sage Foundation had already proved its usefulness to social work and social reform by financing the Pittsburgh Survey and by assisting the National Tuberculosis Association begin its educational exhibits. The Rockefeller Sanitary Commission, organized in 1909 and later absorbed by the Rockefeller Foundation, demonstrated that hookworm disease could be eradicated. In the course of this campaign the Commission advanced the entire movement for public health. The General Education Board co-operated with the Department of Agriculture in efforts to increase the productivity of southern agriculture. The Board made valuable contributions to secondary education in the South and to higher education in all parts of the country. The Carnegie Foundation for the Advancement of Teaching inaugurated pensions for college teachers which furthered interest in pensions for other workers, and it sponsored and published Abraham Flexner's epochal *Medical Education in the United States and Canada* (1910). As early as 1912 Edward T. Devine denied that foundations would inhibit the normal springs of benevolence. On the contrary, said Devine, the effect of the foundations had been to stimulate both public appropriations and private giving for education, health, and welfare.

"You have had the best run for your money I have ever known," Elihu Root once told Andrew Carnegie. Carnegie, a cheerful and impulsive giver in spite of his theories, managed to dispose of $350 million. John D. Rockefeller, less impulsive than Carnegie, also had a good run for the $530 million he conferred on benevolent causes. "We must always remember that there is not enough money for the work of human uplift and that there never can be," he said in 1909. "How vitally important it is, therefore, that the expenditure should go as far as possible and be used with the greatest intelligence!" The advice, although sound, was commonplace. It was the application that was difficult. Rockefeller's and Carnegie's chief contribution to philanthropy was to found institutions capable of distributing private wealth with greater intelligence and vision than the donors themselves could hope to possess. The great philanthropic trusts they established climaxed the long effort to put large-scale giving on a businesslike basis.

VIII

The Business of Benevolence and the Industry of Destruction

> I suppose we had to do it, and I suppose it was worthwhile, but think of the creative job we could have done with that money in a world of reason and sanity!
>
> GEORGE E. VINCENT

While administrators of great wealth were devising new methods to dispose of surplus millions, promoters of good causes offered the general public unparalleled opportunities for relieving pockets and bank accounts of spare dollars. And what a variety of goods "retail philanthropy" displayed! Churches, home and foreign missions, temperance organizations, church-related or non-sectarian colleges, hospitals, orphanages, and homes for the aged always needed money. The plight of newsboys, working girls, distressed immigrants, tenement dwellers, and southern mountain children was held up for all to see. Disasters at home or abroad brought appeals for aid from the Red Cross and special relief committees. In good times and bad local relief associations, charity organization societies, settlement houses, babies' milk funds, free dispensaries, children's aid societies, societies for the prevention of cruelty to children and animals, the Y.M.C.A., Y.W.C.A., Y.M.H.A., Salvation Army, and Volunteers of America advanced their respective, and separate, claims for support.

Opportunities and importunities for giving, already numerous in 1900, increased enormously in the next decade and a half. The continuing vitality of the voluntary principle and a broadening sense of responsibility for improving the social environment led to the formation of a host of new national organizations maintained by dues, donations, and subscriptions. These were the years when the Boy Scouts, Girl Scouts, Campfire Girls, National Tuberculosis Association, American Cancer Society, Goodwill Industries, the Lighthouse, National Association for the Advancement of Colored People, National Urban League, American Association for Labor Legislation, National Child Labor Committee, and a hundred other leagues, associations, and committees came into being. Incomplete as the listing is, the names suggest the diversity of interests supported by private giving. After 1914 the situation was further complicated by the necessity of relieving war-sufferers in Europe.

In 1914 American philanthropy, if judged by the standards of a Rockefeller, Carnegie, or Morgan, was still conducted in a distressingly unbusinesslike way. This was less true of the internal operation of philanthropic agencies, many of which were professionally managed and efficiently organized, than of the relations of the different societies to each other. Both locally and nationally benevolent activities were poorly coordinated. Partly because of the rapid expansion in the prewar years, partly because of the nature of voluntary enterprise, there was duplication or overlapping of effort, rivalry for public favor, competition for funds. Fund-raising in particular was in a chaotic condition. As Mathew Carey had pointed out many years earlier, those who gave were solicited time and again, while many potential givers were either ignored or approached in ways not calculated to stimulate generosity.

These defects were obvious to social workers, and progress toward correcting them was being made before the war. Even in a nation of joiners social workers displayed remarkable ability to find or create organizations to join. They formed conferences within conferences, and established federations, councils, and committees to improve and promote special fields and methods of social work. In a few cities representative councils of welfare agencies took over the task, earlier attempted by charity organization societies, of raising standards and co-ordinating charitable efforts. Federated fund-raising, first tried in Denver in 1888, realized among Jewish charities in Boston in 1895, and adopted in a broader scale in Cleveland in 1913, was shortly afterward put into effect in fifteen other cities. Meanwhile a Danish innovation, the sale of special stamps at Christmastime to "stamp out" tuberculosis, had been taken up in the United States. After 1910 when the Christmas seal campaign became a joint responsibility of the Red Cross and the National Tuberculosis Association, it proved a relatively painless method of raising money and also demonstrated the possibility of co-operation between national voluntary agencies. Sums raised in Christmas seal campaigns ($450,000 in 1913) were small, however, compared to those garnered each year by the Y.M.C.A. The Y.M.C.A.'s leadership in fund-raising went back to the days of the evangelist, Dwight L. Moody, but in the decade after 1905 practice made near-perfect the hard-hitting, highly publicized "Y" drive to attain a specific dollar goal in a limited period through professionally directed teams of volunteer collectors.

Of all American philanthropic organizations the American Red Cross, by tradition, the terms of its charter, and international agreements, was most directly concerned by the outbreak of war in Europe. In 1914 the Red Cross had fewer than 150 chapters and only about twenty thousand members; but even these modest figures reflected an appreciable growth in size and strength in the decade since the reorganization that accompanied Clara Barton's resignation. Its unofficial leader from 1905 to 1915 was Miss Mabel Boardman, a woman of inherited wealth, established social position, high ideals, and fixed opinions who, in making the Red Cross a national organization, shaped it after her own comely image. When war came, Miss Boardman and Red Cross officials promptly offered assistance to sister societies in Europe and called on the chapters to raise funds for war relief. At the time (August, 1914) and for more than a year thereafter, Miss Boardman and her advisers interpreted Red Cross charter obligations strictly and assumed that war relief could legally be extended only to sick and wounded combatants. In September, 1914, amid fanfares of publicity, a Red Cross "mercy ship" sailed for Europe bearing 170 doctors and nurses and supplies and equipment to establish hospital units in the warring nations. Partly because of the expense involved in maintaining these units, they were withdrawn in October, 1915, but, to the extent that the Allied blockade permitted, the Red Cross continued to send medical and hospital supplies to the fighting forces of both sides.

In fact, as events in the very first months of the war proved, medical assistance for combatants was much less needed than relief to civilians in occupied countries, to refugees from war zones, and to sufferers from disease and famine caused by military destruction, blockade, and the disruption of normal life. Belgium was the immediate problem. There, in the space of a single month, an industrious, thriving, populous nation was reduced to destitution, its industry, trade, and transportation destroyed. By autumn, with stores and warehouses empty, and factories closed, almost the entire population, numbering some 7,500,000, was in desperate straits. On October 16, 1914, Brand Whitlock, the American minister in Brussels, cabled President Wilson, "In two weeks the civil population of Belgium, already in misery, will face starvation." That Belgium did not starve was due almost entirely to the efforts of an unofficial, unincorporated organization set up in London about a week after Whitlock sent his message to Wilson.

The Commission for Relief in Belgium grew out of an attempt made by a Belgian relief committee to buy food in England. The Belgian group sent Millard K. Shaler, an American mining engineer then living in Brussels, to London to make the purchase. In London, Shaler sought out another mining engineer, Herbert Hoover, who had recently won fame by directing the relief and repatriation of thousands of American travelers stranded in Europe at the start of the war. When British officials refused to grant Shaler a shipping permit for the goods he had bought, Hoover and Shaler appealed for assistance to Ambassador Walter Hines Page. In co-operation with other neutral diplomats, Page obtained a guarantee from Germany that Belgian relief supplies would not be requisitioned by the occupation forces and arranged with Allied governments to allow those supplies to pass through the blockade. And, with the help of a Quaker conscience, Hoover made a wise decision. He exchanged a $100,000-a-year business career for the difficult and unremunerated post of chairman of the Commission for Relief in Belgium, a step which was to lead him, leap by leap, into positions of helpfulness and power such as few men have known.

The task of the C.R.B. was to acquire, by purchase or gift, the tons upon tons of food and clothing needed to sustain the people of Belgium, and later of German-occupied portions of northern France; to assemble and transport these supplies from all over the world; and, as a neutral agency, to oversee their distribution or sale (to those who could afford to buy) by Belgian and French relief committees. In the best of circumstances the task would have been immense, and the difficulty of performing it in the midst of war can scarcely be imagined. Fortunately, in addition to the brilliant leadership of Hoover and his staff—which included, among others, a contingent of Rhodes Scholars—the C.R.B. had the co-operation of the belligerents and the warm support of world opinion. In the two and a half years of American neutrality no philanthropic cause found wider favor in the United States; but supplies and money came from other countries, too, and in proportion to population New Zealand made the largest contribution. The Commission could not have accomplished its work, however, had it depended solely on voluntary contributions of philanthropic individuals or groups. All told these amounted to about $52 million, while the monthly expenditures of the Commission ran from $5 million at the outset to a high of $30 million in 1918. By far the greater part of the approximately $1 billion spent by the C.R.B. between November, 1914, and August,

1919, came from Belgian government funds on deposit abroad, subsidies by the British and French governments, and, after 1917, United States government loans. After the United States entered the war the work of the Commission continued under Dutch and Spanish sponsorship.

One of the agencies which assisted the C.R.B. at the start of its operations was the Rockefeller Foundation. The Foundation, just beginning its mission of promoting "the well-being of mankind throughout the world," had not contemplated entering the field of direct relief. It had intended to "go to the root of individual or social ill-being or misery" and had assumed that its proper work lay in the advancement of public health through medical research, education, and demonstration. Nevertheless, in the autumn of 1914 the Rockefeller Foundation provided a depot for the use of the C.R.B., purchased almost a million dollars worth of food for the Commission, chartered ships, and advanced funds for freight charges. Meanwhile, the Foundation appointed a War Relief Commission, headed by Wickliffe Rose, who had been in charge of the Rockefeller Sanitary Commission's campaign against hookworm, and including Ernest Bicknell, on leave from his position as national director of the American Red Cross. This Commission investigated relief needs in all the nations at war, established a European headquarters in Switzerland, conducted a variety of relief programs on its own, and provided funds to assist other agencies in their work.

In all, one hundred and thirty American agencies were participating, directly or indirectly, in war relief at the end of the period of American neutrality. They had sponsored activities ranging from sewing classes for Belgian refugees in Holland to educational, recreational, religious, and welfare services of Y.M.C.A. secretaries in prisoner-of-war camps. The Red Cross conducted a successful campaign against typhus in Serbia in 1915 and, at the end of that year, reversing its earlier policy, became active in civilian relief. The American Committee for Armenian and Syrian Relief raised money to feed and shelter refugees in Turkey, Persia, and Russia; and the American Jewish Relief Committee attempted against insuperable odds to get aid to Poland, where hundreds of thousands of civilians—facing the same problem as the Belgians —perished from disease and starvation. Nowhere were humanitarian efforts conducted on as large a scale or as generously supported as in Belgium. Even there, and to a much greater extent elsewhere, the tightening Allied blockade—which at last declared contraband even such items as rubber gloves for surgeons—interfered with the flow of supplies. Voluntary philanthropy was at best but a feeble weapon to oppose the engines of war, and all that could be done by American agencies met but a minute part of an overwhelming need.

James T. Shotwell, general editor of the *Economic and Social History of the World War* (a 150-volume work which was not completed until the eve of World War II), observed in 1929 that the most remarkable thing about the war was not that it involved so many people but that it involved them so completely. For Americans the period of total involvement was far shorter than for other major participants. Brief though the experience was, it accelerated and accentuated tendencies that were to give twentieth-century American civilization a distinctive character. This was as true of philanthropy as of other aspects of American life.

The changes worked by war were most obvious in the American Red Cross. In April, 1917, President Wilson summoned a conference of businessmen and financiers to discuss the financing of the Red Cross war program. These men promised the Red Cross increased support from the business community, providing its administration was strengthened by appointment of a War Council. In May, 1917, the War Council occupied the newly completed national headquarters building and transformed the Red Cross from an agency of neutrality and humanity into an auxiliary of the United States armed forces. The War Council selected as its chairman Henry P. Davison, a member of J. P. Morgan and Company, and he in turn named other leading bankers, corporation executives, and, inevitably, a public relations expert, to top positions in the organization. At the time of Davison's appointment it had been said that he was the kind of man who could make the Red Cross a "50 million dollar proposition instead of a 5 million dollar one." Davison did more than that. One of his first decisions was to set the goal for the 1917 fund drive at $100 million.

This figure—a sum fifty times as large as the Red Cross had spent for war relief between 1914 and 1917, and much larger than any voluntary organization had ever before attempted to raise—is as good a symbol as any of the daring and vision Davison brought to the Red Cross. The campaign to obtain it was no simple appeal to chapters for funds. It was a carefully planned undertaking to convince the public that every dollar given to the Red Cross was a demonstration of patriotism and a contribution to victory. To assist in conducting the campaign the Red Cross borrowed Charles S. Ward, the Y.M.C.A.'s most successful money-raiser, and seventy-five experienced Y.M.C.A. secretaries. Campaign leaders, working with amazing speed, assigned quotas to individual cities and towns, rallied community and business leaders to the cause, organized thousands of volunteer workers, and prepared the countless forms, posters, advertising layouts, and publicity releases to be used in the drive. Conducted in June, hard on the heels of the First Liberty Loan, the campaign not only achieved but exceeded the goal. Similar methods applied with more time for planning carried the 1918 drive to the astonishing total of about $175 million. In all the Red Cross collected $400 million during the war and postwar years, and membership, which stood at about a quarter of a million at the start of 1917, had reached twenty-one million by the start of 1919.

With vastly increased funds and members the Red Cross was in a position to render effective assistance both to American troops and to civilians and fighting men in the Allied countries. From the outset aid to the Allies, especially France, loomed large in Davison's program for the Red Cross. The organization ultimately spent considerably more in assisting refugees, children, the families of French soldiers, and the French anti-tuberculosis campaign than in services for the American Expeditionary Force. In World War I the Red Cross supplemented Army and Navy medical departments much more directly than in World War II. It recruited men for the ambulance corps and nurses for the Army, Navy, and Public Health Service; and set up, equipped, staffed and sent overseas numerous base (1,000-bed) hospitals and smaller hospital units.

While the Red Cross had exclusive responsibility for supplementary relief for the sick and wounded, it shared responsibility —that is, competed with—a number of other philanthropic agencies in serving able-bodied soldiers and sailors. The Commission on Training Camp Activities maintained some semblance of order in the United States by permitting the Red Cross to distribute supplies and perform social work through field directors attached to military units, and authorizing the Y.M.C.A., Knights of Columbus, Jewish Welfare Board, War Camp Community Service, and Y.W.C.A. to develop educational and recreational services in camps and surrounding communities.

Overseas, however, the situation was more confused because the Army did not attempt to co-ordinate the work of the private societies engaged in military relief. The agencies themselves, eager to be helpful and anxious to prove the worth of their services, set up hotels, clubs, canteens, "huts," and "dugouts" wherever they could, jockeyed for position and favor, and became embroiled in unwholesome religious and institutional rivalries. The result was spotty and uneven service, some areas being oversupplied with facilities, while others received not so much as a baseball, chocolate bar, or magazine from the societies. Agencies like the Y.M.C.A. which attempted to do most suffered criticism for sins of omission and commission; those like the Salvation Army which attempted relatively little won extravagant praise. In the long run the confusion and competition produced by what Raymond Fosdick of the Commission on Training Camp Activities called "the present policy of laissez faire" was to convince the Army that the morale services attempted by the societies should not be left to private agencies. "Morale," as Fosdick stated in his final report to the Secretary of War, "is as important as ammunition and is just as legitimate a charge against the public treasury."

The competition of the private agencies extended from the field of action to the crucial area of fund-raising. Here, how-

The Business of Benevolence

ever, the pressure of public opinion and the influence of Secretary of War Newton D. Baker and John D. Rockefeller, Jr., eventually forced the seven national organizations (other than the Red Cross) that were participating in soldier relief at home and abroad to join in a united fund drive. The United War Work campaign of November, 1918, although inaugurated amid impressive demonstrations of unity, was conducted under peculiarly difficult conditions. The great influenza epidemic, which reached its peak in October, was still in progress and incapacitated both solicitors and contributors. More important, the war was coming to an end. John R. Mott, the saintly secretary general of the Y.M.C.A. stepped into the breach with the startling message that peace was more dangerous than war. "We need not be solicitous for our soldiers and sailors when they are drilling and fighting and confronting the great adventure of life and death," he announced. The real danger and need lay ahead when relaxation of discipline and more leisure would expose the troops to increased temptations. A nation in the process of adopting the Prohibition amendment responded enthusiastically to this and similar moral arguments. Moreover a 1917 amendment to the income tax law encouraged individual giving by permitting deduction of charitable contributions up to 15 per cent of taxable income. This provision, combined with the 60 per cent surtax levied on high incomes, enabled the very rich to give generously of money that would otherwise have gone to the Collector of Internal Revenue. Once again the goal was oversubscribed. In what was then called "the largest voluntary offering in history," the United War Work Fund raised $200 million "to prevent the period of demobilization becoming a period of demoralization."

Peace in truth did present problems, and problems much

graver than the leisure-time activities of American soldiers and sailors. The chief problem was to get food, clothing, and medicine to millions of men, women, and children in central and eastern Europe who were suffering from the worst famine in three hundred years. Fortunately the United States had quantities of agricultural commodities which it was more than willing, for humanitarian, economic, and political reasons, to send abroad. If helping suffering humanity also helped American farmers dispose of surplus corn and wheat, so much the better. The important thing was that assistance was needed and provided in enormous quantities.

Throughout most of 1919 European relief needs were far greater than voluntary agencies could meet. This was the period when Mr. Hoover, simultaneously head of the United States Food Administration, Grain Corporation, American Relief Administration, and also director general of relief for the Allied governments, performed his most remarkable feats of financing and executing international aid. Toward the end of 1919, while governmental relief agencies were being liquidated, American philanthropy assumed the task of feeding and caring for millions of European children left orphaned, crippled, homeless, and undernourished by war and attendant catastrophes. At the suggestion of Mr. Hoover, who had transformed the once official American Relief Administration into a private charitable organization, the numerous groups interested in this field organized the European Relief Council; the Council conducted a joint fund drive in the winter of 1920–21 to which foundations, school children, and community chests contributed $30 million.

Cotton Mather's observation that the reward of doing good is an increase in opportunities to be helpful was borne out

The Business of Benevolence

later, in 1921, when the Russian writer, Maxim Gorki, appealed to "all honest European and American people" for food and medicine for famine-stricken Soviet Russia. Previous proposals to send aid to postrevolutionary Russia had come to naught because of suspicion on both sides. However, in the summer of 1921 Mr. Hoover, now Secretary of Commerce but acting in the capacity of chairman of the unofficial American Relief Administration (the beneficiary of the assets of the Grain Corporation, which Hoover had headed during the war), was able to negotiate an agreement with Russia. The Soviets agreed to give A.R.A. personnel freedom, protection, and assistance in relief operations, and the A.R.A. undertook to extend such assistance as it could and guaranteed that its workers would not participate in political activities. The Russian and American governments, the A.R.A., the Red Cross, and organizations as various as the Volga Relief Society, Southern Baptist Convention, American Friends Service Committee, and Laura Spelman Rockefeller Memorial helped finance the program. A businesslike undertaking conducted to the mutual satisfaction of both the Soviet government and the A.R.A., Russian famine relief constituted a hopeful precedent for the future as well as a successful capping of the international relief activities of the war era.

Nearly all the foundations contributed heavily to the war and postwar fund drives. In the sentence quoted at the head of this chapter George E. Vincent of the Rockefeller Foundation expressed the point of view of foundation executives: war relief was necessary and presumably worthwhile, but it was not the creative job that the foundations hoped to perform. Education and research were the real concerns of foundations, and even during the war they continued active in these fields.

American Philanthropy

Public health, medical research, and medical education—all three, of course, closely related—were the particular interests of the Rockefeller philanthropies. Between 1913 and 1929 the International Health Commission of the Rockefeller Foundation, operating on a world-wide scale and always working in co-operation with governmental agencies, lent its assistance to campaigns against hookworm, yellow fever, pellagra, malaria, and tuberculosis. Foundation philanthropy is often regarded as impersonal, but four scientists serving the Rockefeller Foundation, including the renowned bacteriologist Hideyo Noguchi, died of yellow fever while fighting that disease in Africa or South America.

The Rockefeller Foundation and the General Education Board, in what was perhaps their most important service, made large grants to medical schools in the United States and abroad. The key figure in obtaining and distributing the $50 million which Rockefeller contributed to the cause was Abraham Flexner (1866–1959), secretary of the General Education Board for a decade after 1917. Funds supplied by Flexner, whom Hans Zinsser dubbed "the uncle of modern medical education in America," were not free gifts, but hardheaded investments, made on condition that the recipient would raise an equal or larger sum from other sources and institute improvements in facilities and instruction. The emphasis was on improving the quality rather than on expanding the number of medical schools. Through the assistance of these grants, and as a result of the stimulating effect they had on giving by other donors and appropriations by state legislatures, medical education—backward and neglected in 1910—had been virtually revolutionized by the end of the 1920's.

The Business of Benevolence

A more difficult task, and one much less completely effected, was improvement and expansion of educational facilities for southern Negroes. "The only purpose for which the Negro has asked or received philanthropic aid has been for the support of education," said Booker T. Washington in 1912. Northern philanthropists had been furnishing this aid ever since emancipation. At the turn of the century, interest in the education of Negroes merged with the efforts of the Southern Education Board and the General Education Board to promote the public school movement in the South. "We have no thought of colonizing northern teachers in the South, or of propagating northern ideas at the South," said Wallace Buttrick of the General Education Board to a joint session of the Georgia legislature; "quite the contrary; we believe that . . . your schools must be organized and maintained by you in harmony with your institutions and traditions." This approach was based on the philosophy that progress in the education of Negroes depended on further education of southern whites. In practice it meant acquiescing, at least for the time being, in the development of segregated and unequal school systems. But Negro education, although subordinated to white, was not entirely neglected. Philanthropy continued to provide opportunities for Negro youth that southern states and communities could not or would not undertake on their own initiative. In the two decades after 1911 Julius Rosenwald of Sears, Roebuck, and Company, through various personal gifts and grants made by the Rosenwald Fund, contributed to the building of more than five thousand rural schools. Toward the end of the 1920's the Rosenwald Fund, the General Education Board, the Carnegie Corporation, several other foundations, and Negro philanthropists (such as James and John Burrus of Nashville) displayed greater interest than formerly in higher education for Negroes.

Two events at the end of the war—the doubling of Yale's endowment through the Sterling bequest and Harvard's successful, professionally directed campaign to raise $14 million—augured well for higher education. In the next decade foundations and individual donors, including Edward S. Harkness, George Eastman, and James B. Duke made conditional or outright gifts to colleges and universities that enlarged endowments, created new departments, altered the appearance of campuses, and (in the case of Duke) changed the name of the institution. The Carnegie Corporation gave so exuberantly in the early 1920's that by 1924 it had pledged $40 million in future income to various institutions. Conditional grants made by the General Education Board had by 1925 added an estimated $200 million to the endowments of three hundred institutions. A newer development, fostered by the growth of foundations, was the promotion of scholarship by means of fellowships and grants for advanced research. Some foundations were operating agencies, conducting investigations and performing services through their own staffs. The larger number, however, were fund-dispensers and used part or all of their income to finance studies undertaken by individuals or groups independent of their control. The latter course, as the Rockefeller Foundation early learned, was especially necessary in controversial areas, such as the social sciences, where the objectivity of the investigation must be clearly demonstrated.

Even in the 1920's questions were raised whether foundation-financed research could be objective and whether institutions accepting aid from foundations and corporations could maintain their integrity. There was a flare-up of the old tainted-money debate in 1925 when the board of regents of the University of Wisconsin, in an action both praised and derided, resolved not to accept gifts from "incorporated educational endowments"—although it continued to accept donations from the Wisconsin Manufacturers' Association, public utility companies, and other corporations. Generally speaking, however, scholars were more interested in securing adequate support for research than in quibbling about its source; and obtaining funds from foundations for fellowships, grants-in-aid, and other research subsidies became one of the tasks of the American Council of Learned Societies and the Social Science Research Council. In addition to research projects of individual scholars, foundations supported such large-scale co-operative ventures as the *Encyclopedia of the Social Sciences* and the *Economic and Social History of the World War*. It was not a foundation, however, but the New York Times Company which financed preparation and publication of the original twenty volumes of the *Dictionary of American Biography;* and it was a private citizen, John D. Rockefeller, Jr., who gave the Library of Congress $500,000 to begin the enormous task of reproducing material relating to American history in the archives of foreign countries.

Whether performed by great donors such as Mr. Rockefeller, Jr. (whose personal benefactions included gifts for the resurrection of Colonial Williamsburg and toward the restoration of Versailles, Reims Cathedral, and Fontainebleau), or by men and women of lesser means, individual giving remained the mainstay of philanthropy. Foundations had increased to two hundred by 1930 and annually poured millions of dollars into selected channels of benevolence. Their aggregate endowment, however, approximately $1 billion, was only about half what Americans gave each year for philanthropic purposes. Habits of giving and techniques of raising money developed during the war continued in the 1920's. Each year the springs of charity poured out a golden flood: $1.75 billion in 1921, $2 billion in 1924 and 1925, almost $2.5 billion in 1928.

During the 1920's the business of benevolence developed professionals, not only in the arts of casework, but in the specialty of fund-raising. The former were notoriously underpaid; the latter were well rewarded for their services. Social workers, influenced by contemporary trends in psychiatry and interested in techniques of helpfulness, became increasingly concerned with complex problems of individual adjustment to social stress. Professional fund-raising companies counseled and otherwise assisted fund-seeking institutions to reach their goals, charging a flat fee or a percentage of the collection. By the end of the 1920's there were twenty firms of this sort in New York City alone; their clients included leading colleges, churches, and community chests.

Spurred by the success of the war drives, the community chest movement spread from 40 cities in 1919 to about 350 a decade later. At the outset federated financing had been opposed both by strong agencies which had no difficulty in raising money and by those who saw in it another example of business domination. Acceptance of the community chest idea, which of course was by no means complete, reflected the force of the "New Era" concept of co-operation in all areas of enterprise. The community chest reduced competition and promoted rational distribution of charitable profits. It expanded the number of givers, increased the amount of money available for social work, and ultimately released social agencies from dependence upon a few well-to-do givers. The chest, sometimes called "the budget plan of benevolence," made giving less an act of personal charity than a form of community citizenship, almost as essential as the payment of taxes.

The outpouring of money for philanthropy was matched only by the praise heaped on it. From time to time, it is true, doubts were expressed about the wisdom of undue reliance by society upon private benefactions. But critics of business civilization seldom questioned American generosity and defenders frequently boasted of it. In 1928, a year which saw five hundred lump-sum gifts of $1 million or more, the *Saturday Evening Post* characterized the charitable zeal of business leaders as a "practical application of the golden rule." "We work, and we work hard, not for the money itself but for the good that may be done with it," said the *Philadelphia Inquirer* early in 1929. And a sober historian, Marcus W. Jernegan, writing in a learned journal in March, 1929, affirmed the popular view: "Never in the world's history have such unprecedented amounts of money been granted by private and public agencies to alleviate human suffering."

Professor Jernegan's inclusion of public agencies was significant. Even before the depression public expenditures for welfare were growing more rapidly than private contributions to charity. State after state had adopted special relief programs for dependent children, the blind, and the aged. State appropriations for mental hospitals and schools for blind and deaf children increased; so also did local outlays for public health nursing, baby clinics, dispensaries, hospitals, and sanatoriums. Nevertheless, at the very crest of prosperity, aid to the needy was already straining the budget of family welfare societies. In April, 1929, the *Survey Graphic* devoted an entire issue to problems raised by what was then called technological unemployment. All too soon—although not soon enough—the normal business of benevolence would yield the stage to the grim business of relief.

IX

A Time to Remember

*The effort to make voluntary charity solve the
problems of a major social crisis . . . results only
in monumental hypocrisies and tempts selfish people to regard themselves as unselfish.*

REINHOLD NIEBUHR

Almsgiving, a practice long out of fashion in philanthropic
circles, came back into style in the first two years of the great
depression. Little was heard in 1930 and 1931 of the old warning that an excess of benevolence would debauch and pauperize
the poor, although a great deal was said about the soul-destroy-
ing effects of governmental doles. Financiers and corporation
executives threw themselves into the work of raising funds for
the unemployed and discovered, as one of them said, "There's
a spiritual side to helping those who must have help this
winter." Industrialists lent warehouses for use as shelters for
the homeless. Al Capone, Y.M.C.A.'s, newspaper publishers,
and Catholic nuns supported breadlines. A society woman—
so the story went—admiring the breadline run by Mrs. X,

"Lady Bountiful of the Bowery," said to a social worker: "Please find out what it costs. I'd love to have one."

These charitable labors were carried on with the blessings of the President of the United States. No one was more disturbed by the paradox of poverty in the midst of plenty than Herbert Hoover. No earlier President recognized as fully the responsibility of the federal government to take vigorous action to promote economic recovery. And none of his predecessors was more firmly convinced that responsibility for relieving distress lay with individuals, voluntary organizations, and local governments. In speech after speech Hoover sought to drive home the obligation of individuals and communities to prevent those "in honest difficulties" from suffering hunger and cold. Time and again he attempted to stimulate the nation's spiritual energies to greater charitable efforts. "Charity is the obligation of the strong to the weak," he said in February, 1930. "Works of charity are the tests of spiritual development of men and women and communities." As the months and years passed, Hoover's praise of charity, "the loftiest of all spiritual qualities," became more fulsome. His speeches usually included some reference to "community service" or "mutual self-help" through the responsibility of local government, but he never waxed as eloquent about tax-supported assistance as about voluntary benevolence.

The President's approach placed heavy burdens on community chests and the American Red Cross. The former, in Hoover's opinion, stood for the sense of charity in individual cities; the latter, which he called "one of the most beautiful flowers of the American spirit," represented "our people in their most generous, unselfish and spontaneously warm-hearted character." Both institutions, to the best of their abilities, lived up to the trust the President imposed in them. Community chests in a number of cities, including hard-hit Detroit, reached their goals in the autumn of 1930 and in some instances raised larger sums than in previous years. "In every city," reported the Association of Community Chests and Councils in November, 1930, "a large part of the increase has come directly from job-holders—persons who may at any time have to turn to the chest for aid." Meanwhile, in one of the most curious and characteristic episodes of the early depression period, the American Red Cross spurned a proposed congressional grant of $25 million and undertook to relieve two and a half million drought sufferers in twenty-three states with $5 million from its disaster reserve funds and $10 million raised in a special campaign. "All we pray for is that you let us alone and let us do the job," the chairman of the Red Cross central committee told Congress in January, 1931.

President Hoover enthusiastically indorsed the Red Cross's rejection of the government's tainted money. The immediate problem was famine, but, as he saw it, the basic moral issue involved was vastly more important. "We are dealing with the intangibles of life and ideals," Hoover said. "A voluntary deed by a man impressed with the sense of responsibility and brotherhood of man is infinitely more precious to our National ideals and National spirit than a thousandfold poured from the Treasury of the Government under the compulsion of law." Statistically minded critics estimated that the Red Cross drought-relief program, the largest peacetime operation in which it had ever engaged, brought those aided an average of 42 cents of assistance per week.

As the depression worsened and the nation, in the President's words, passed through another Valley Forge, the administration launched its most ambitious effort to alleviate distress through benevolence. In August, 1931, Hoover announced the appointment of Walter S. Gifford as head of the Organization for Unemployment Relief. Gifford, described by *Time* as "a 'clean desk' executive" whose only hobby was charity, was president of the American Telephone and Telegraph Company and also of the New York Charity Organization Society. To assist Gifford in the task of mobilizing and co-ordinating the charitable resources of the country Hoover enlisted the services of one hundred leaders of business, industry, finance, and philanthropy. The organization distributed model relief plans to cities and towns across the nation and prepared a nationwide campaign to raise an undisclosed sum—unofficially reported to be $175 million—for community chests and other private relief agencies. By an unfortunate coincidence United States Steel, Ford, General Motors, and other large corporations— many of whose executives were members of the President's Unemployment Relief Organization—announced wage-cuts of 10 per cent or more just before the campaign was scheduled to begin. In the circumstances Hoover's speech opening the fund drive sounded even more cloistered than usual. He dwelt on the "God-imposed responsibility of the individual man and woman to their neighbors" and urged Americans to be their brothers' keepers.

No fund appeal since the war drives of 1917 and 1918 received wider publicity or had a more professional flavor than the campaign of October–November, 1931. Movie theaters and college football teams gave benefit performances. Radio broadcasts carried messages of inspiration and hope to millions of homes. Advertising agencies contributed a series of high-powered advertisements which appeared, free of charge, on billboards and in newspapers and magazines. If anything the campaign was oversold. Although there were no representatives of the unemployed in the President's Relief Organization the first advertisement purported to be an open letter from "Unemployed, 1931." Tightening his belt, as well he might, "Unemployed, 1931" said, "I'll see it through if *you* will!" The second proclaimed, "Between October 19th and November 25th America will feel the thrill of a great spiritual experience." Give liberally, the copy writer urged, "And know that your gift will bless yourself; it will lift your own spirit." Another advertisement, which looked very much like those for toothpaste, declared, "The world *respects* the man who lives within his income. But the world *adores* the man who *gives* to the LIMIT of his ability." Finally, "In one month . . . every city and town in the land will raise the funds that will be necessary to banish from its borders the fear of hunger and cold. . . . Just one month, and our biggest job will be over."

Twenty years later Hoover recorded in a volume of his *Memoirs* that the drive was a success both in raising funds and in "awakening" a sense of national responsibility for being " 'my brother's keeper.' " Contemporary evidence and opinion, although divided, was less reassuring. The campaign did raise a great deal of money, but the total was closer to $100 million than $175 million, and this was nowhere nearly enough to banish from the nation either the fear or the actuality of hunger and cold. Those who chose could take comfort from the fact that 200 community chests, reached or slightly exceeded their quotas and 179 increased previous totals by 14 per cent. On the other hand, those who were so inclined, and they included the executive director of the Association of Community Chests and Councils, could point out that one-fourth of the chests had failed by 10 per cent or more; that only 35 per cent of chest funds would be spent for relief and that this represented only 30 per cent of the total conservatively estimated need for relief in the chest cities. The other 70 per cent was supposed to come from tax-supported agencies. Chest success did not accurately reflect a community's ability to meet the crisis, since exhausted resources or limitations on taxing and borrowing powers made it impossible for many cities to raise the public share of relief funds. In practice a chest goal was more likely to be an estimate of the amount which could be raised than an indication of the sums really needed by welfare agencies. Moreover, the campaign had no effect on sorely distressed rural areas, mining villages, and mill towns where there were no local charities and only the most rudimentary public provisions for poor relief.

While the campaign receipts were still being totaled, a Senate committee began hearings on two bills proposing federal appropriations for unemployment relief. Mr. Gifford was unable to provide the committee with definite information on the extent of unemployment, the number of persons in need, the number then receiving aid, or the standards of assistance furnished the needy. He gave the impression, however, that matters were well in hand. With unintended humor he observed that federal appropriations might be a disservice to the unemployed, since "Individuals would tend to withdraw much of the invisible aid they are now giving."

A number of social workers also appeared before the Senate committee. These witnesses, in close touch with the relief situation in their communities, were much less confident than Mr. Gifford that matters were well in hand, and they were less disturbed by the prospect of federal aid. Two years of depression had wrought changes in social workers' thinking. There was no tendency now to magnify the extent of private benevolence or to dwell on the superiority of charity to public relief. On the contrary, witness after witness maintained that even in normal times private organizations relied on public agencies to carry the major burden of assistance and that in the present emergency it was public responsibility and public appropriations, not private giving, that required stimulation. Walter West, executive secretary of the American Association of Social Workers, testified that the country's existing relief system was primitive. It forced the jobless and their families to bear almost the entire cost of unemployment, since neither public nor private agencies relieved them until they were destitute. One advantage of federal relief, said West, would be to "take off some of the curse of charity." Another witness, J. Prentice Murphy of Philadelphia, advised the committee: "If the modern state is to rest upon a firm foundation, its citizens must not be allowed to starve. Some of them do. They do not die quickly. You can starve for a long time without dying."

Hoover's speech opening the emergency fund drive had implied that philanthropy was on trial. Actually the trial was over. Philanthropy stood condemned, convicted not only of bankruptcy but of more heinous offenses. The fact that private relief organizations, Red Cross chapters, and religious groups such as the American Friends Service Committee were doing what public bodies found it impossible or inconvenient to do received little notice. Philanthropy, according to its critics, was a dodge of the rich to escape taxes and hold on to power. This was an old charge that gained new force each time business tycoons asked others to be their brothers' keepers. "Riot insurance" was the name scoffers gave the businessmen's and bankers' relief efforts. Theodore Dreiser, who had once written with weird objectivity of the curious shifts of the poor now, in *Tragic America* (1931), denounced all charity as a racket, controlled like everything else by Wall Street. Paul Douglas, Stuart Chase, and other liberal economists marveled at the mentality of men who abhorred the "dole" of unemployment insurance and cherished breadlines, handouts, and relief drives as the American Way. It remained for Abraham Epstein, a pioneer crusader for public old-age insurance to commit the supreme heresy. He denied that Americans were generous. In a widely quoted article published in the *American Mercury* in 1931 Epstein declared: "The myth of our unparalleled generosity has no firmer base than the benevolence of a very few men who have distributed small parts of their extraordinarily large fortunes."

That Hoover's homilies on charity should have contributed to bringing philanthropy into disrepute was unfortunate, ironic, and understandable. History abounds in examples of humanitarians who were ahead of their times. Hoover belonged to a different breed: the humanitarian behind the times. In his public addresses he seemed to envisage American society as a sentimental jungle in which the overflowing hearts and tender consciences of the strong would minister everlastingly to the wants of the weak. He revered charity too highly and attached too much virtue to casual giving—so much, in fact, that he was tempted to place the interests of the benevolent before the needs of the necessitous. Possibly because of experience in war and famine relief he tended to equate philanthropy with succor of the suffering. This was an old and respectable view, and tenable in time of war or natural disaster. It was not adequate or appropriate, however, in an era of economic crisis; and it conflicted with a long-established tendency in American philanthropy. For years Americans had boasted of their generosity but almost in the same breath they had decried the need for charity. The constant effort of American humanitarians since the days of Cotton Mather had been to restrain and discipline, not to expand, the charitable impulse. With the assistance of great givers like Carnegie and Rockefeller they had sought and all but succeeded in turning the main stream of philanthropy from ameliorative to preventive and constructive tasks. It was too late to reverse the direction. As the governor of New York observed in August, 1931, the time for platitudes had passed.

To the despair of friends and foes Franklin D. Roosevelt usually managed to avoid either getting too far ahead of or lagging too far behind public opinion. In his attitudes toward charity, as in so many other matters, he revealed an understanding of abiding tendencies in the national character. Instead of exaggerating the moral significance of neighborly kindness, he attempted to prove, as Tocqueville would have said, that virtue was useful. Even in acknowledging gifts to a favorite charity, the Warm Springs Foundation, Roosevelt went to some pains to point out that every disabled person restored to useful citizenship added to the assets of the nation. "By helping this work," he said, "we are contributing not to charity but to building up of a sound nation." Similarly, in calling for state aid to the unemployed in 1931, Roosevelt declared that such help should be offered "not as a matter of charity, but as a matter of social duty." Subsequently he was to defend vast federal appropriations for unemployment relief as a means of promoting business recovery; and still later he argued that federal minimum wage, maximum hour, and child labor laws were necessary to conserve manpower, increase purchasing power, stabilize markets for farmers' products, and make business more profitable. Ironically enough, Roosevelt's insistence —sometimes strained and occasionally comic—on finding practical justifications for humanitarian action appears to have been an important factor in convincing an adoring electorate that his heart was in the right place.

Under Roosevelt's leadership New York became the first state to offer assistance to local governments in the financing and administration of unemployment relief. A number of other states followed New York's example but in others timidity, disinclination to burden taxpayers, constitutional prohibitions, and in some cases sheer lack of resources precluded effective state action. Nevertheless a break had been made with the outdated assumption that relief was a purely local responsibility. After that not even the Chamber of Commerce of the United States and an organization called Sentinels of the Republic (which sponsored a series of radio broadcasts in which prominent conservatives addressed the nation on "Too Much Government," "Government Interference in the Home," "The Menace of Paternalism," and "Our Vanishing Freedom") could block the drift toward federal participation in relief. Hoover stood firm as long as he could. But in the spring of 1932 he asked the Red Cross to supervise the processing and distributing of surplus wheat and cotton to the needy—a task which the organization accepted and performed with dispatch and credit—and in July he gave his approval to a measure authorizing the Reconstruction Finance Corporation to make grants thinly disguised as loans to state for unemployment relief and public works. After Roosevelt entered the White House the tentative steps already taken in the direction of greater governmental responsibility for welfare turned into something resembling a march. The tempo varied from time to time but generally the movement went forward.

When the emergency was over—it lasted for the better part of ten years and was ended only by the greater crisis of World War II—the nation had not only survived but in doing so had entered a new social era. The ransoming of capitalism had cost more money than any government had ever before spent in time of peace. Enormous expenditures for public welfare required borrowing on a scale that only war had previously justified, and the adoption of a revenue program that compelled wealthy persons and large corporations to carry a larger share of the tax burden than they were accustomed to bear. As a result of grants-in-aid to states and federally administered work and relief projects the unemployed were better provided for than in any previous depression. Admittedly this was not saying much. Social workers, not to mention the unemployed and the so-called unemployables, recognized needs which, if they had been met, would have required still larger appropriations than Roosevelt and his oddly assorted supporters were willing to sanction. It is significant that both at the time and later the New Deal was as often criticized for attempting too little as for doing too much. In all likelihood a comparable emergency in the future will be met by prompter and more, rather than less, governmental action.

Incomplete though the New Deal relief and security programs were, they registered a striking advance over the inhumane, archaic, and unsystematic methods of treating distress practiced before the depression. By 1941 the United States had a start toward social insurance systems that would protect workers against some of the hazards of age and unemployment.

It had a considerable start toward federal-state partnership in caring for the aged, the blind, and dependent children. Federal leadership, supervision, and financial assistance had strengthened the states' welfare services and had encouraged states to adopt measures such as unemployment insurance which they had previously been hesitant to put into effect. Preventive measures to forestall or minimize dependency and promote security had been inaugurated, had been approved by the Supreme Court, and had seemingly become accepted as permanent obligations of government. Most surprising of all, in the midst of depression, organized labor had grown in numerical strength, legal status, and aggressiveness. Assisted by the generally sympathetic attitude of the federal government, larger numbers of Americans than ever before had won and were vigorously exercising the right to improve their economic conditions through collective bargaining.

The entry of the federal government into relief financing and the consequent expansion of public welfare activities at all levels of government took some of the pressure off philanthropy. Throughout the 1930's there remained ample need for the services private agencies could offer millions of families on relief and the millions more who, although hardpressed, were not yet receiving relief. No one pretended, however, that private charity played more than a subordinate and supplementary role in the alleviation of distress, and the common assumption was that its responsibilities in this area would continue to decline. Philanthropy was almost rid of the unwelcome task of relieving destitution and almost free to return to more congenial occupations: "pioneering," development of experimental programs, promotion of research, enrichment of cultural life, and improvement of techniques of helpfulness applicable to individuals and families at any income level.

The only problem was money. "Where are the millions of the 1920's?" was a familiar lament. The springs of charity by no means dried up, but they ran at only about half their usual volume. The stock market crash reverberated through the corridors of art galleries and music halls, for even in normal times museums, symphony orchestras, and opera companies operated at a deficit and relied heavily on a few very rich and generous patrons. Proud organizations like the New York Philharmonic and the Metropolitan Opera Company now had to pass the hat to ordinary music lovers. Saving the "Met" became almost a yearly event, nearly as exciting as opening night. The Red Cross, the National Tuberculosis Association, and hundreds of private agencies represented in local community chests retrenched.

Even richly endowed foundations felt the squeeze of hard times. The Julius Rosenwald Fund, for example, could not meet pledges made when the market was high; its endowment was invested in common stock of Sears, Roebuck, and Company, which dropped from $200 a share in 1928 to $10 in 1932. The Fund was saved from premature liquidation by the cooperation of the General Education Board and the Carnegie Corporation, which took over some of its responsibilities, and by changing its program from making grants to engaging in research. Other major foundations, although not as seriously affected by the depression, also adjusted programs to meet the emergency. Grants became smaller and more varied and were directed more toward fellowships and support of specific research projects than to increasing institutional endowments.

The Carnegie Corporation, like the Rosenwald Fund, operated under the burden of commitments made in freer spending days. Nevertheless, the Corporation was able to contribute almost $2 million to emergency relief and social service agencies in 1932–33, and throughout the depression period it found the means to assist art museums and to promote art and musical education. The Carnegie Corporation also supplied the American Foundation for the Blind with funds to develop recorded or "talking books" for those of the blind who could not use Braille (about 80 per cent). The venture offered a classic example of the way philanthropy is supposed to work, because in 1935, after the foundations had perfected the program, Congress began to appropriate money to the Library of Congress to permit nationwide extension of the service.

The depression caught the Rockefeller Foundation in the throes of reorganization and in the midst of replacing old leaders with new. The new officials were less medical-minded than their predecessors, more willing to support research in the social sciences and humanities, and less averse to "scatteration," the foundation expression for retail philanthropy. In 1933 the trustees appropriated a million and a half dollars to expedite discovery of remedies for the depression. No very striking results flowed from this emergency measure, but the grants the Foundation made to the National Bureau of Economic Research and similar agencies contributed to advances in methods of studying economic problems as well as to the accumulation of more precise knowledge of income distribution and related issues. Hardly less valuable, in a time of increasing governmental responsibilities, was the Foundation's aid to the Public Administration Clearing House. This agency, still operating in Chicago, brought together organizations representing public officials in city management, welfare, public works, finance, and personnel administration. The Rockefeller Foundation bore out its claim to be a pioneering institution by lending support to the extension and improvement of instruction in the Russian, Chinese, and Japanese languages in the early 1930's, long before the necessity for such work was popularly recognized.

Despite the scaling-down of benefactions as the economic crisis became more serious, some of the millions and some of the millionaires of the 1920's remained active in the 1930's. Several of today's larger foundations, including the A. W. Mellon Charitable and Educational Trust (1930) and the Kellogg (1930) and Sloan (1934) Foundations, came into being during the darkest years of the depression. The great individual givers, Edward S. Harkness and John D. Rockefeller, Jr., while contributing generously to emergency relief drives, also gave on an even more generous scale to the kinds of projects in which they had long been interested. Harkness, like the younger Rockefeller, devoted his life to disposing of the fortune his father had made in Standard Oil. His princely gifts went to princely institutions: Harvard, Yale, Columbia, Phillips Exeter, Lawrenceville School, the Metropolitan Museum of Art, and great hospitals and medical centers. Rockefeller's benefactions rivaled his father's in size and outdid them in variety. The restoration of Williamsburg, the colonial capital of Virginia, International House at the University of Chicago, the Cloisters Museum, and preservation and development of park sites from Mt. Desert Island and New York City to the Grand Tetons were among his philanthropic interests in the early 1930's.

Restoration projects also appealed to the master tinkerer,

Henry Ford. His attitude toward charity— "Give the average man something and you make an enemy of him"—smacked more of the cracker barrel than of the gospel of wealth, and it was a cracker-barrel world that Ford attempted to reincarnate at the Ford Museum and Greenfield Village in the industrial city of Dearborn, Michigan. The Museum was a replica of Independence Hall that spread over acres and contained relics of old-fashioned ways of doing business, making things, and going places. Surrounding the Museum was Ford's reproduction of an early American village. It revealed, in one fascinating, inharmonious whole, the birthplaces of Ford, Noah Webster, William A. McGuffey, and Luther Burbank, a seventeenth-century stone cottage from England, a steamboat from the Suwannee River, the schools Ford had attended as a boy, a tintype studio, a windmill from Cape Cod, a village green, a colonial church, Thomas A. Edison's workshop and laboratory, the Wright brothers' cycle shop, and the building in which Ford had built his first automobile. Opened in June, 1933, the Museum and Village enshrined themselves in the hearts of countless visitors whose country was even then moving ahead, so Franklin D. Roosevelt said, toward the goal of a self-supporting and self-respecting democracy.

Philanthropy could survive the depression. But could it survive the New Deal? That was the question conservatives worried about, especially after the advent of the new and more aggressive New Deal labor, social security, and tax policies of 1935. Community chest leaders scored a victory that eventually proved to be important when, over Roosevelt's mild objections, they amended the Revenue Act of 1935 to permit corporations to deduct charitable contributions up to 5 per cent of taxable income. Those who professed to believe

MORALE

It wins wars.

It beats depressions.

It lays the firm foundations for prosperity.

AMERICA is engaged in a mighty enterprise of morale building. In one month—October 19th to November 25th—every city and town in the land will raise the funds that will be necessary to banish from its borders the fear of hunger and cold.

Just one month, and our biggest job will be over. Just one month, and we shall have met the worst threat the Depression can offer; and we shall have won!

You can help. Give to the funds that your community is raising. Give generously.

Feel the thrill that comes with victory. Go forward with America to the better days ahead.

The President's Organization on Unemployment Relief

Walter S. Gifford
Director

Committee on Mobilization of Relief Resources

Chairman

The President's Organization on Unemployment Relief is non-political and non-sectarian. Its purpose is to aid local welfare and relief agencies everywhere to provide for local needs. All facilities for the nation-wide program, including this advertisement, have been furnished to the Committee without cost.

Advertisement of the President's Organization on Unemployment Relief. (From *The Saturday Evening Post*, November 14, 1931.)

Scene in ARC Roosevelt Club, Manila, 1946. (Reproduced by courtesy of American National Red Cross.)

that business was conducted for no other purpose than to support charities continued to express grave doubts about the effect of higher estate, income, and corporation taxes on giving, and about the implications for philanthropy of the New Deal's allegedly leveling tendencies. Soon there will be no more millionaires, ran the argument. With the goose will go the golden egg. And then what will happen to churches, colleges, museums, and hospitals? The *Saturday Evening Post* warned that government might go on piling up taxes but it need not expect benefactions to pile up too. As if to prove the point the widely publicized will of Jesse Isidore Straus, president of Macy's department store and former chairman of the New York State Temporary Relief Administration, contained a codicil revoking gifts to eighteen philanthropic institutions because of high estate taxes levied by the state and federal government.

As events were to prove, it was possible for both benefactions and taxes to pile up. Since the days of Amos Lawrence large donors had been in the habit of describing their charitable gifts as investments; in the face of higher income and inheritance taxes, the richer the donor, the sounder his charitable investments became. The economic uses of philanthropy were not exploited to the full until the war prosperity of the 1940's. Even in the 1930's, however, it was recognized that a person in the higher income brackets, if so inclined and properly advised, could make useful contributions to philanthropy with little sacrifice of spendable income, and occasionally to his own advantage. In making income tax returns donors could deduct charitable gifts up to 15 per cent of taxable income; they could avoid the capital gains tax by giving appreciated stock to a foundation or recognized philanthropic institution (and, as trustee, continue to vote the stock); and they could reduce the amount of inheritance taxes their heirs would have to pay by bequeathing judicious portions of their estates to incorporated foundations. It was also possible, as Edsel and Henry Ford demonstrated, to arrange matters so that the foundation would pay the inheritance tax imposed on the portion of the estate left to members of the family.

Philanthropy remained in bad repute in liberal and radical circles throughout the 1930's, and for reasons which, if not new, were vigorously and cogently argued. "Philanthropic and business interests are not merely complementary, they are identical," observed one critic in 1938. "Just as you can't run a steel mill without machine guns, so you can't run a capitalist democracy without a pretense of philanthropy." Eduard C. Lindeman, of the New York School of Social Work, whose *Wealth and Culture* (1936) was a study of the operation of one hundred foundations during the 1920's, offered an economic interpretation of modern philanthropy: it was disintegrating capitalism's way of distributing, in its own interest, wealth which could not be spent on luxuries, was not needed for reinvestment, and could not profitably be employed for speculation. Foundations, and by implication all large-scale benefactions, denoted the development of a rudimentary social consciousness in the donors, but they also represented the donors' determination to control social thought and expression. Lindeman's judgment of the trustees of the great philanthropic foundations was even more damning than his interpretation of the motivation of donors. Taken as a group the trustees represented "social prestige, financial success, and middle aged respectability." These were exemplary attributes, but were they adequate or proper qualifications for leaders of organizations supposedly dedicated to pioneering, pathfinding, opening-up of new frontiers of social well-being? Lindeman did not think so. "Nothing," he said, "is so repugnant as the arrogance of those who presume to impose cultural norms upon a society on no basis of warrant other than . . . pecuniary success under . . . a competitive economy."

Since Americans have seldom been disposed to obey the proverbial advice to refrain from looking gift horses in the mouth, it is not surprising that in the 1930's, of all times, they should have cast wary and suspicious eyes on the benefactions of millionaires. The gifts were accepted but with slight thanks. In 1936 the *Christian Century*, recalling Charles Lamb's fable, reflected that to perpetuate the present system in order to keep up the flow of million-dollar gifts would be like burning down a house to roast a pig. The *Nation* observed in 1934 that the best thing that could happen to American universities would be an inability to find rich men to beg from and to put on their governing boards. The broker Charles Hayden's bequest (1937) of $50 million to endow a foundation for educating American youth mentally, morally, and physically prompted the *New Republic* to remark, "If these are the best uses to which vast fortunes can be put it might be better not to permit such accumulations at all." "It is a good thumping gift but it is not enough to justify the existence of swollen fortunes," Heywood Broun said in 1937 of Andrew Mellon's offer to give the federal government both his collection of old masters and the money to house the collection.

Mellon's gift, announced in December, 1936, was a thumping big one indeed, the biggest single benefaction of the decade, and the largest gift that had ever been made to the United States government. The grand total for the collection, the

National Gallery building, and an endowment fund contributed by the Mellon Educational and Charitable Trust was in the neighborhood of $80 million. There was no disposition to reject Mellon's offer but the fact that the aging financier had made it while a suit involving his 1931 federal income tax return was pending received due, or perhaps undue, notice. In the spirit of the time critics deplored the conservative design of the gallery building and worried lest the self-perpetuating board of trustees might discriminate against living American artists. The National Gallery, which opened in 1941 *was* classic in style, but its permanent collection contained works by living American artists as well as masterpieces by dead Europeans. The Index of American Design, a gift of the federal government, comprised 20,000 water colors and drawings of folk and decorative arts prepared by artists employed on WPA art projects.

There were other evidences of the New Deal's patronage of the fine arts, music, drama, scholarship, education, and recreation. Not only in relief but in many other fields the taxpayer of the late 1930's was supporting activities once regarded as primary concerns of the philanthropist. But larger governmental expenditures, instead of stifling neighborly kindness, seemingly stimulated it. As early as 1935 the nation's total contribution to private benevolence, estimated as $2.5 billion, slightly exceeded the pre-depression peak. By 1938, in spite of conservative fears and radical jeers, philanthropy again ranked as one of the leading American enterprises.

If material as well as spiritual considerations contributed to the revival of private giving, it was nevertheless true that philanthropy emerged from the depression decade with a stronger base of popular support. The number of contributors to community chests rose even when chests failed to reach their goals. Annual Mobilizations for Human Needs, the nationally conducted publicity campaigns for community chests, were carried out with all the fervor and dedication of war drives—which in fact they soon became. The Red Cross experienced no difficulty in raising a $25 million relief fund at the time of the Ohio-Mississippi floods of 1937, and, in furnishing assistance, did not hesitate to work with numerous federal agencies, including the W.P.A. and the C.C.C. The President's Birthday Balls and the March of Dimes campaigns of the National Foundation for Infantile Paralysis brought philanthropy into the hearts and price-range of the multitudes. Those who disdained traditional charity had abundant opportunity to contribute time and again to committees, leagues, and alliances fighting militarism, fascism, racial injustice, and violations of workers' rights.

As the 1930's drew to a close, philanthropy still faced difficult problems. It had lost its sentimental aura and it remained to be seen whether the public could be induced to give as generously for preventive and constructive tasks as for emergency relief of suffering. It also remained to be seen whether philanthropy could, in fact, provide the leadership, imagination, and understanding necessary to devise happier social relationships. Meanwhile, as Roosevelt observed in paying tribute to the work of volunteer and official agencies in the floods of 1937 and the New England hurricane of 1938, there was no conflict between private and governmental welfare service. There was more than enough work for both, he said, not only in meeting disasters, but in "our national effort to lift up the lower one-third of our nation to a standard of living that will conform with decency and comfort and self-respect." Before that task was completed another war and a continuing emergency widened the horizons of both government and philanthropy. The problem was not one-third of the nation, but something like one-half of the globe.

X

A Voyage Is Now Proposed

A voyage is now proposed to visit a distant people
on the other side of the globe; not to cheat them,
not to rob them, . . . but merely to do them good,
and make them, as far as in our power lies, to live
as comfortably as ourselves.

BENJAMIN FRANKLIN

World War II was an expected war in which the United
States was not expected to participate. War had been so often
forecast and so long anticipated that the German invasion of
Poland in September, 1939, came almost as an anticlimax. A
decade of crises had familiarized the world with the politics of
terror, violations of treaties, subversion of established governments, seizure of foreign territories, and bombing of civilians.
In the prewar years and continuing at least until the middle of
1940, American policy, as expressed in neutrality legislation,
official statements, and public opinion polls, was to deplore aggression and to affirm that the mistake of 1917 would not be
repeated. Whatever happened American boys would not be

sent overseas to fight other nations' battles. Munitions makers, international bankers, and foreign propagandists would not again be permitted to draw the United States into a war to save democracy.

In this climate of opinion philanthropic efforts to relieve victims of war and oppression multiplied but rarely flourished. Throughout the 1930's American Jews gave unstintingly to finance the Joint Distribution Committee's far-flung, desperate labors to save Europe's persecuted Jewry from extinction. Pacifist, youth, and church groups tirelessly solicited for China and Spain. "We dance that Spain may live," read placards announcing dances sponsored by college students sympathetic to the Loyalist cause. There was no lack of organizations seeking funds for overseas relief. The trouble was that they all appealed to the same relatively small segment of the American people who were genuinely concerned about Fascist aggression. Attempts to obtain broader popular support made little headway. In 1938 the American Red Cross tried and failed to raise $1 million for Chinese relief. The Committee for Impartial Civilian Relief in Spain had even less success in attempting to collect $300,000 so that the Red Cross and the American Friends Service Committee might supply limited quantities of surplus American foodstuffs to both sides in the Spanish Civil War. The events of 1939 brought little change in public attitudes except to heighten suspicion of actions which might conceivably endanger the neutrality of the United States.

The Neutrality Act of 1939, adopted shortly after the outbreak of the war, recognized the possibility that the overseas operations of American relief organizations might affect the foreign policy and national interests of the United States. The

Act, in addition to numerous restrictions on American economic activity in nations officially declared to be at war, required voluntary agencies which wished to engage in civilian war relief in belligerent countries to register with and submit monthly reports to the Department of State. The Act specifically excluded the American Red Cross from the registration and reporting provisions and it did not apply to agencies operating in nations such as China, the Soviet Union, and Finland, which were not technically belligerent. During 1940 and 1941 the number of both registered and unregistered foreign relief agencies increased rapidly as the war spread to more and more countries. In the approximately two years of American neutrality in World War II, about seven hundred American organizations raised a total of $90 million for civilian and refugee relief overseas, and Congress appropriated an additional $50 million for distribution to refugees by the Red Cross. The fall of France in the summer of 1940 made assistance to nations still fighting the Axis powers seem less a form of charity than one of the measures "short of war" contributing to the defense of the United States.

At the same time that agencies for overseas civilian relief were increasing in number (there were seventy for Great Britain alone), national defense measures at home brought a boom in domestic welfare services. Aid to American armed forces, only recently in bad repute, regained its traditional popularity after adoption of the Selective Service Act of 1940. "Swing into patriotic note," the vice-chairman of the Red Cross advised chapter leaders in the autumn of that year. Early in 1941 the Red Cross swung into the blood donor program, its major contribution to national defense and one of the notable achievements of voluntary activity in the war years.

Meanwhile, profiting from experience in World War I, the Y.M.C.A., Y.W.C.A., National Catholic Community Service, National Jewish Welfare Board, Salvation Army and National Travelers Aid Association combined their military welfare programs and fund appeals in the United Service Organization for National Defense (U.S.O.).

Unfortunately the co-operative approach represented by U.S.O. was the exception rather than the rule in 1941. Groups in every community wanted to do something for the draftee and were determined to do it by themselves. There were no bottlenecks in the organization of war charities. The President's Committee on War Relief Agencies, appointed in 1941, studied the problem of duplication and encouraged combination of agencies engaged in the same or similar lines of work. The Committee, however, lacked authority to exercise effective supervision. The war relief picture, confused before Pearl Harbor, became chaotic afterward. By the summer of 1942 the President's Committee reported that the number of war relief agencies could only be estimated, that those operating in the domestic field were subject to no co-ordination, supervision, or control, and that the public was therefore subjected to far too many solicitations by agencies which duplicated work performed by others. "We were fairly falling over each other in a complex and undirected effort to organize, to publicize, to solicit, and to give," recalled Winthrop Aldrich, who was president of the British War Relief Society and active in U.S.O.

By an executive order issued in July, 1942, President Roosevelt transformed the earlier Committee on War Relief Agencies into the President's War Relief Control Board and greatly increased its authority. The Board now had power to control all solicitations for voluntary war relief, both foreign and domestic; only the American Red Cross, church, and other non-war charities remained outside its jurisdiction. It had power to license and withdraw licenses from war relief agencies and, in the interest of economy and efficiency, to eliminate or merge organizations. The Board scheduled the various national fund appeals and prevented competing campaigns during the periods set aside for the Red Cross, National War Fund, United Jewish Appeal, and War Bond drives. The staff of the Control Board sharply scrutinized overhead costs and made reasonable economy of operation a requirement for continued licensing. It found that in a few agencies overhead costs consumed 50 per cent, 70 per cent, and in extreme cases, all of the funds raised for relief. When the members of the Board (Joseph E. Davies, Charles P. Taft, and Charles Warren) made their final report in 1946, they could point to impressive achievements: the Board had cut the number of war relief agencies from seven hundred to ninety had promoted a remarkable degree of co-operation among the survivors, and had improved the services they offered. It had played a part in reducing overhead costs from an average of 10 per cent in 1942 to just over 3 per cent in 1945; and it had helped bring the National War Fund into existence.

The National War Fund, a private non-profit corporation established late in 1942, was the most ambitious venture in united fund-raising the United States had yet seen. In three national campaigns conducted in 1943, 1944, and 1945 the Fund combined the appeals of local non-war charities (mainly community chests) and the major war-related service and relief agencies including U.S.O., British War Relief, United Service to China, and American Aid to France. The union of war and non-war charities was fortunate for all concerned. Local welfare organizations, which might otherwise have suffered from the competition of the more glamorous war agencies, received considerably more than half of the $750 million total raised in the three War Fund drives. "The chests had the organization, and the war agencies had the appeal," the general manager of the National War Fund later remarked; "as long as the war lasted it was a winning combination."

Even while this winning combination was operating, it was obvious that larger funds than voluntary organizations could muster would be required for postwar relief. In November, 1943, fifty governments organized the United Nations Relief and Rehabilitation Administration (UNRRA) in a co-operative effort to meet the immediate postwar needs of war-devastated countries. At the close of the war this international agency sold or gave the governments of liberated countries immense quantities of food, clothing, medical supplies, livestock, and other relief materials. To the extent that it was possible to do so UNRRA returned exiles, prisoners, and refugees to their homes. For those who could not or dared not go home it operated displaced persons camps. UNRRA was financed by the non-invaded countries which provided commodities and cash to the extent of 2 per cent of their national incomes in 1943. The United States share of the $4 billion expended by UNRRA was $2.6 billion. In addition to money and goods from governments UNRRA received $210 million in cash, clothing, food, and livestock from individuals and associations in the United States, Canada, Australia, and New Zealand. Needless to say, this hopeful experiment in sharing resources on the basis of "from each according to his means and to each according to his needs" did not survive very long in a divided, distrustful world. UNRRA lasted long enough, however, to tide nations in bitter need over the worst of the postwar crisis and to help avert widespread famine and epidemic.

Neither the work of UNRRA nor the lend-lease and economic recovery programs launched by the United States government during and after the war diminished the eagerness of the American people to extend sympathetic assistance to people in foreign countries. After 1943 the American Council of Voluntary Agencies for Foreign Service, comprising the larger foreign relief agencies registered with the President's Control Board, planned and co-ordinated non-governmental programs. CARE, the Cooperative for American Remittances to Europe (later Everywhere), which began sending food parcels from Americans to designated recipients overseas in 1946, was one of the Council's creations; CRALOG (the Council of Relief Agencies Licensed to Operate in Germany), LARA (Licensed Agencies for Relief in Asia), and ARK (American Relief for Korea) were others. All of these alphabetical agencies, as their names indicated, were federations of numerous organizations which pooled their energies for a common cause.

The bureaucratic character of postwar relief was the product of several factors: the number of people and organizations wishing to help, the hard realities of fund-raising, and the extraordinary complexities of relief operations after 1945. Programs had to be approved by and correlated with those of official agencies. In occupied areas clearance had to be obtained from military authorities. Elsewhere, agreements had to be negotiated with governments regarding protection of property, exemption of relief supplies from customs duties and other taxes, and freedom from ration control. These difficulties, however, did not prevent fifty or more voluntary agencies from entering the field. Between September, 1939, and December, 1945, American voluntary agencies sent more than $500 million in goods and funds to war sufferers overseas; in the six years after the war private philanthropy raised approximately $2 billion for relief, reconstruction, and social services abroad. The aid furnished by voluntary organizations, impressive though it was, was insignificant in comparison to the appalling need. Nevertheless it reflected the light of American kindliness and good will, a candle if not a beacon in the stormy night.

Philanthropic contributions to postwar relief supplemented the much larger expenditures made by official agencies. In the period immediately after the war the American army spent as much as $500 million a year for civilian relief in countries where United States troops were stationed. Under the Marshall Plan, or European Recovery Program, which began in 1948 and continued until 1951, the United States helped nations of western Europe bolster their economies by means of grants and loans totaling $12.5 billion. The Marshall Plan was a form of prudent investment rather than a display of loving kindness and even ardent supporters of tax-supported foreign aid acknowledged that "person to person" giving possessed virtues that "government to government" assistance could never attain. Parcel post packages sent to friends and relatives in foreign countries accounted for a large share of personal giving. CARE and religious organizations such as the Roman Catholic War Relief Services and the Protestant Church World Service provided additional channels through which private citizens contributed relief supplies to individuals, churches, and charitable institutions overseas. In 1946 American Jews, numbering less than five million, collected $105 million for the

United Jewish Appeal, and in 1948 they raised $150 million for it. With funds supplied by U.J.A. the Joint Distribution Committee, United Palestine Appeal, and United Service for New Americans took European Jews out of displaced persons camps, assisted Jewish emigration and resettlement, and helped the new state of Israel in its fight for life.

War needs and war prosperity contributed in about equal measure to the generous support accorded assorted philanthropic causes in the 1940's. War taxes, although reaching levels which might reasonably have been expected to inhibit voluntary giving, did not in fact have that result. Charitable contributions reported in income tax returns were five times as large in 1945 as in 1939; corporation gifts increased nine times during these same years. Possibly the amounts given to charity might have been larger if taxes had been lower, but in the opinion of J. K. Lasser, the nation's favorite income tax adviser and author of *How Tax Laws Make Giving to Charity Easy* (1948), the taxing system fostered "the natural impulses to give to charity." The tax laws recognized the necessity and desirability of private contributions to charitable, religious, and educational institutions by permitting individuals and corporations to make tax-deductible gifts for philanthropic purposes. Progressive rates virtually assured that persons whose incomes were subject to surtaxes and corporations in the excess profit bracket would make contributions at least up to the limit of tax deductibility. For wealthy people and profitable corporations charity was a bargain, because what was given was mainly forgiven taxes. In the upper income brackets the question became not whether one could afford to give but whether one could afford not to give. It was not necessary for large givers to seek "tax loopholes" in order to take advantage of the inducements the revenue code offered donors. Their benefactions, although hard on the Treasury Department and presumably burdensome to other taxpayers, accorded with the letter and spirit of the law.

Income, inheritance, and corporation taxes, which continued at a high level in the decade after World War II, also contributed to a great increase in the number of foundations, one of the striking philanthropic developments of the postwar and Cold War era. Out of consideration for the social utility of foundations the revenue code conferred various privileges upon them. Subject to certain restrictions, foundation income from investments was tax exempt; contributions to foundations were deductible; and the gifts and bequests they received were subject neither to gift nor estate taxes. Quite aside from tax benefits, the foundation provided a convenient method of channeling the gifts of large individual and corporate donors to beneficiaries; with tax advantages, and in the face of high income and estate taxes, the foundation was irresistible. In the late 1940's there was evidence that some foundations served the donors' business interests better than they served philanthropy. In 1948 a congressional investigation conducted by Senator Charles W. Tobey of New Hampshire uncovered some of the curious uses to which foundations might be put. They could and were being used to provide venture capital for industry, to safeguard dynastic control of business enterprises, and to permit ruthless operators to plunder and wreck going concerns. Of course the unscrupulous businessman could not pocket the foundation's tax-free profits but, as trustee, he could use them for further piratical ventures. As one observer noted, there might even be something left over for occasional gifts to charity.

A Voyage Is Now Proposed

Separating foundation goats from foundation sheep was not easy, and eradicating those which were simply tax-evasion schemes without hurting legitimate foundations was even more difficult. A complicated revision of the revenue code adopted in 1950 dealt with the worst abuses. Under the new law, foundations might lose tax-exempt status if their records showed they existed mainly for the accumulation of capital or if they engaged in certain transactions which diverted income or principal to the donor or his associates. In any case income obtained by conducting a business unrelated to the foundation's ordinary purpose was subject to taxation. Nevertheless the legal or not yet prohibited forms of tax benefit enjoyed by foundations remained sufficiently appealing to encourage further growth. By the mid-1950's their number exceeded 5,000 by conservative estimate and approached 7,500 by some counts.

In the early 1950's the larger and more reputable foundations, whose financial affairs were conducted with such probity that they expressed willingness to operate in a fishbowl, were subjected to a different kind of scrutiny. Had they made grants to support un-American or subversive activities? If so to whom? When? Why? How much? Since government offices, universities, public schools, churches, motion picture studios, and radio and television networks were under attack for harboring subversive elements, and since philosophical systems, methods of scholarship, textbooks, folk tales, and works of art were widely suspected of spreading un-American attitudes, it was only natural that foundations should also be subjected to congressional investigation.

There were two probes. The first, held in 1952 under the auspices of the Select (Cox) Committee of the House of

Representatives, asked the larger foundations to answer a searching 100-item questionnaire, and through public hearings, interviews, and correspondence gathered additional material on foundation operations. The Committee reported that in a few instances foundations had made grants to individuals or associations subsequently "cited or criticized" by congressional committees, but that the general record of the foundations was good. The second or Special (Reece) Committee investigation of 1954 was less judiciously conducted. Its chairman, paid staff, and practically all the witnesses permitted to testify reiterated that foundations, educational institutions, and research organizations were involved in a "diabolical conspiracy" to foist socialism on the American people. By a majority vote the Committee ended the hearings without permitting the foundations to reply, except through written statements. In a minority report two members of the Committee called the proceedings "an ugly stain" on the record of the House of Representatives. Whatever disservice the Committee rendered the House, it did no serious harm to foundations. Editorial reaction to the Reece Committee was distinctly unfavorable. Foundations were already unpopular with extreme rightists; nobody else took the majority report seriously—least of all, apparently, one of the members of the Committee who accompanied his signature of the report with a statement expressing disapproval of its principal findings and conclusions.

Foundation officers have long maintained that it is extremely difficult to give money away wisely. In the late 1940's and 50's they did not suffer from lack of advice. Edwin R. Embree, formerly president of the Rosenwald Fund and an old Rockefeller Foundation hand, warned the foundations against "scatteration." William H. Whyte, Jr., the anti-organization

man, reminded them of their obligation to support the individual researcher. The Cox Committee made it plain that foundations were expected to check on the "loyalty" of scholars, musicians, artists, and research institutions before making grants to them. Seymour Harris, a distinguished economist, advised foundations and non-profit research organizations to avoid public policy issues and to concentrate on collecting and organizing facts. Congressman B. Carroll Reece, who regarded "empiricism" as a dangerous, un-American "ism," wanted to know why foundations did not support "pro-American projects" such as "studies regarding the excellence of the American Constitution, the importance of the Declaration of Independence, and the profundity of the philosophy of the Founding Fathers"? William H. Whyte, writing in *Fortune*, a comparatively safe platform from which to make the suggestion, urged foundations to exercise "their ability and will to contribute to changes in the status quo of American life." All these recommendations implied dissatisfaction with current foundation practices. The most serious was Edwin Embree's charge that foundation giving was becoming "conventional and stereotyped" and that there was "an ominous absence of that social pioneering that is the essential business of foundations."

The principal recipient and target of this advice and criticism was the Ford Foundation, which was the newest face and had the fattest purse in the foundation world. Although organized in 1936, the Ford Foundation concentrated on local and family affairs until after the death of Henry Ford in 1947 and did not become active nationally until the early 1950's. Then, in possession of 90 per cent of the stock of one of the nation's greatest corporations, it was in a position, and necessarily

obligated, to spend on a larger scale and broader front than any other foundation. Its resources, counted in billions rather than millions, comprised one-third of the combined assets of all foundations, and by 1954 its annual appropriations represented between a fourth and a fifth of total foundation spending.

The most striking thing about the Ford Foundation was its announced decision to spend money "in the difficult and sometimes controversial task of helping to realize democracy's goals." This meant problem-solving, not in the relatively safe and approved areas of medical and biological research, but in the social sciences, education, and the field of international understanding. To solve its own problem of rapidly accumulating funds the Foundation set up a number of autonomous organizations such as the Fund for the Advancement of Education, Fund for Adult Education, Fund for the Republic, Resources for the Future, Center for Advanced Study in the Behavioral Sciences, and the National Merit Scholarship Corporation. Some of the Foundation's direct grants for research in the social or behavioral sciences supported teams of scholars engaged in efforts to solve problems which, in the opinion of critics, were scarcely problems and hardly worth solving. On the other hand the Foundation's largest gift—the largest ever made by a foundation—was universally praised. This was a special appropriation of $560 million announced in December, 1955, to assist privately supported colleges and universities to raise teachers' salaries, to help privately supported medical schools strengthen instruction, and to enable privately supported non-profit hospitals to extend and improve services. Toward the end of the 1950's, in addition to conducting foreign aid and fellowship programs, supporting experiments in edu-

cational television, and supplying venture capital to both the more and less venturesome areas of scholarship, the Foundation began to make grants to novelists, poets, artists, musicians, composers, and dramatists.

Even after the advent of the Ford Foundation individual donors continued to provide roughly 75 per cent of the nation's total contribution to philanthropy. The foundations' share was about 8 per cent, which was slightly more than the percentage from charitable bequests and somewhat more than that of corporation gifts. The total—half of which went to religion—was unprecedentedly high: $5.4 billion in 1954, $6.7 billion in 1957, and proved to be well in excess of $8 billion in 1960. Of course these amounts would not buy as much in the 1950's as in earlier decades, and they were drawn from and had to be spread over a constantly growing population. On the other hand, some charitable obligations were declining because social insurance, buttressed by industrial health and welfare programs, pension plans, and unemployment benefits had strengthened the economic security of workers and their families. Neither governmental nor private welfare programs actually assured the American people against want, but it was certain that never again would voluntary benevolence be-expected to play the dominant role in relieving sheer economic need. For this very reason philanthropy's role became more complex, and its responsibility for devising and demonstrating helpful services was heavier than ever before.

Private welfare agencies were no longer supported only by the rich and they no longer catered only to the poor. They were community enterprises offering counsel, guidance, and opportunities for growth to people at all economic levels. In a real but new sense the old charity organization motto, "Not alms but a friend," was the program of philanthropy in the 1950's.

Alms, if not being distributed to the needy, were still being collected by a variety of organizations through house-to-house and direct mail solicitations. Some of these were frauds which, in the 1950's, took an estimated $120 million a year from unwary givers. The vast majority, however, were legitimate and a great many had to do with health—or rather disease. It was a rare week (some said night) which did not find mothers marching up and down Main Street armed with collection kits supplied by one or another of the fifty national and innumerable local disease-combating associations. The National Foundation for Infantile Paralysis set the pace, not only in fund-raising but in accomplishing its mission. After scoring a brilliant victory over paralytic polio with the Salk vaccine in 1955, the agency shortened its name to the National Foundation and turned toward the conquest of rheumatic diseases, birth defects, and disorders of the central nervous system.

Social workers and public health experts, without disputing the great service rendered by the National Foundation, American Cancer Society, American Heart Association, and similar groups, questioned whether separate attacks on different ailments added up to an effective program for fighting disease and promoting health. As long as salesmanship and emotional appeal were the tests of support, comparatively rare diseases received as much or more attention than the more serious and prevalent ones. Meanwhile businessmen, labor leaders, newspaper editors, and housewives, became resentful of the ever recurring drives. At the end of the 1950's it seemed probable that the United Fund (a combined community chest and national agency campaign) or some variation of it (such as one

drive for local agencies and another for national organizations)
would sooner or later cut down the number of separate
solicitations by agencies in similar lines of work.

At mid-century the most difficult, vital, and in many ways
most traditional tasks of American philanthropy lay in the
field of foreign aid. Helping those in need wherever they might
be was no new experience for the people of the United States.
The obligation was as old as belief in the stewardship of
wealth and the gospel of doing good. Distance was no barrier
to neighborly kindness in an era of instantaneous communica-
tions and swift travel; and even if Americans had been less
disposed toward benevolence than they were, considerations
of self-interest and national security would have required them
to pay serious attention to the plight of the three-fifths of the
world's population living in near-misery. The poverty of these
people, as President Harry S. Truman warned in 1949, was a
handicap and a threat both to the sufferers and to the rest of
the world.

The "Point Four" program whose outlines President Truman
sketched in his Inaugural Address of January 20, 1949, envisaged a co-operative attack on world poverty through
technical assistance and capital investment in underdeveloped
or overexploited areas. In 1950 Congress implemented the technical assistance features of this "bold new program" by
adopting the Act for International Development. In the Mutual
Security Act of 1957 Congress provided for the establishment
of a new and potentially important lending agency, the
Development Loan Fund. Meanwhile, supported in part
through funds supplied by the United States, United Nations'
agencies such as the Food and Agriculture Organization, World
Health Organization, International Children's Fund, and Inter-

national Bank for Reconstruction and Development, expanded their efforts to help undeveloped areas increase the productivity of their soils and workshops and improve the health and living standards of their people.

This was the kind of work in which American missionaries had been active for a century or longer. At the start of the Point Four program religious organizations and other voluntary agencies were operating approximately 2,500 social service, medical, educational, agricultural, and even industrial projects in Latin America, Africa, the Middle East, and Asia. In the 1950's organized philanthropic efforts overseas (as distinguished from assistance sent by individuals to relatives, friends, and strangers abroad) were co-ordinated by the American Council of Voluntary Agencies for Foreign Service, and mildly supervised by the Advisory Committee on Voluntary Aid (successor to the President's War Relief Control Board), which operated under the United States International Cooperation Administration. In one fairly typical year, 1956, private gifts for foreign relief totaled $535 million or about 8 per cent of all American philanthropic expenditures. The money was used to sow corn and dig wells in Mexico, develop improved varieties of wheat in Colombia, plant trees in Italy, take mason jars to Greece, found a library school and an institute of business administration in Turkey, set up social work demonstrations in Indian villages, and send fishing equipment to co-operatives in Hong Kong. All these and many other projects undertaken by philanthropy continued in the familiar pattern of encouraging self-help and building ladders for the aspiring. The Rockefeller and Ford Foundations were engaged in this work. So was CARE. But it was significant that a great deal of foreign relief and technical assistance was sponsored by religious groups and conducted by employees and volunteers in the service organizations of the various denominations and faiths.

Quantitatively, American philanthropy played only a minor role in the crusade to promote the economic and social development of the poorer half of the world's population. Attempts to measure philanthropy by monetary standards, however, result either in cynicism or complacency and are bound to be misleading. The relatively small share of foreign aid expenditures borne by voluntary agencies did not accurately indicate either the actual or the potential contributions of philanthropy to the work at hand. Limited budgets, as organizations like the American Friends Service Committee regularly proved, were no barriers to useful service. Voluntary agencies supervised the distribution of American food surpluses. They participated, sometimes on a contractual basis, in technical training and agricultural demonstrations. But, as always, the contribution of philanthropy lay less in specific deeds than in a tendency to influence social policy toward responsible action and humane goals. Religious organizations and periodicals were among the most vocal and vigorous champions of Point Four, and the churches were perhaps the most important influence in building up popular support for foreign economic aid.

During the 1950's, partly as a result of the Korean War and the intensification of the Cold War, governmental spending for "mutual security," or military assistance to foreign countries, consumed the lion's share of appropriations for foreign aid. The Point Four program, however, was not abandoned. In 1957, when the total outlay for foreign aid was $8 billion, roughly 20 per cent or about $1.7 billion was designated for economic and technical assistance. Critics denounced Point

Four as a "giveaway," "global charity," and "compulsory benevolence." Supporters viewed economic assistance as an endeavor in which national self-interest coincided with national idealism and asserted that appropriations for it should be doubled. Others, sympathizing with the objectives of the program, questioned its organization and methods of operation. There was room for wide difference of opinions on these points. Some observers, consciously or unconsciously adopting the point of view of scientific philanthropy, suggested that the multiplicity of governmental, intergovernmental, and voluntary agencies participating in technical assistance, the short-term, project-by-project approach followed by most of the operating agencies, and the confusion caused by lack of central leadership and direction were more serious handicaps than inadequate financial support. At the end of the decade the whole foreign aid program, military as well as economic, was under review by Congress.

The voyage Franklin proposed in 1771 was still, almost two centuries later, a very chancy venture. In addition to and quite as important as the question of support or opposition at home, there was the problem of reception abroad. If those who supplied the money were restless, those who received the assistance were proud, suspicious, fearful of being bought. Since technical assistance was essentially an effort to help people help themselves, its effectiveness depended as much on the initiative of the recipients as on the generosity of benefactors. Yet even with the best of intention on both sides there were complicating factors. Every improvement in health and reduction in mortality in undeveloped areas increased the pressure of population on food supplies. Unless production of food kept pace with increasing population, achievement of decent levels of consumption would be impossible. In spite of problems of this sort one school of thought maintained that modern knowledge made human want obsolete. According to other experts the gap was widening, poorer countries growing relatively poorer, hungry continents becoming still hungrier.

Everyone agreed that the extraordinary needs of the age demanded knowledge as well as good will. It was frequently said that fostering economic growth under conditions of freedom was the most challenging task of the twentieth century. Certainly it was one of the most difficult assignments modern man had consciously attempted. The outcome was admittedly a gamble. Whether the risks involved in the undertaking were greater than the possible consequences of failure to act was an unsettled issue.

As the United States entered the second half of the twentieth century, problems that had formerly troubled a few wealthy philanthropists had become the common concern of all citizens. This was true not only because services previously supported by private benevolence were now maintained by taxation but also because the United States had the largest national and per capita wealth of any nation. In facing the problems of a revolutionary epoch the American people had the advantage of great material resources wrested by labor and intelligence from a once underdeveloped continent. They could draw upon the knowledge and skills acquired, and profit from the mistakes made in three and a half centuries of hard-fought struggle to win justice, education, security, and opportunity for all. The American record abounded in men and women sensitive to the misfortunes of their fellows and willing to make others' causes their own. Americans had a long experience in founding voluntary agencies to perform tasks which individuals could not accomplish alone and which public bodies, for one reason or another, were not able to undertake. They had had long experience with charity, too. They knew that charity was subject to abuse, by the giver as well as the taker, and that the most effective and acceptable form of benevolence was not endless, soul-satisfying almsgiving but sensible efforts to help people become independent and prepared to work out their own destinies.

Important Dates

1601	Statute of Charitable Uses, cornerstone of Anglo-American law of philanthropy, and Elizabethan Poor Law, basis of English and American public poor relief, enacted by Parliament
1630	John Winthrop (1588–1649) preaches "A Model of Christian Charity" to Puritans bound for New England
1638	John Harvard (1607–38) bequeaths library and half of his estate to newly founded school at Cambridge, Mass.
1646	John Eliot (1604–90) begins missionary work among Indians of Massachusetts
1649	Society for the Propagation of the Gospel in New England established by Parliament; rechartered in 1661 and continued to support Indian missions until Revolution
1657	Scots' Charitable Society, first American "friendly society," founded in Boston; reorganized 1684
1675	Massachusetts legislature provides relief for frontier settlers driven from homes by King Philip's War, thus departing from principle of exclusive local responsibility for relief
1682	William Penn (1644–1718) comes to America to launch a "holy experiment"
1702	Cotton Mather (1663–1728) publishes *Magnalia Christi Americana*, one of earliest celebrations of American philanthropy

American Philanthropy

1710   Cotton Mather publishes *Essays To Do Good*, a popular do-it-yourself book

1715–18   Elihu Yale (1649–1721) sends gifts to Collegiate School of Connecticut (chartered 1701); school changes name to Yale College

1727   Franklin and friends organize "Junto," a mutual and community improvement society

1729   First orphan home in present boundaries of United States established at Ursuline Convent, New Orleans

1730   St. Andrew's Society founded in Charleston, S.C., "to assist all people in distress, of whatsoever Nation or Profession"

1731   Anthony Benezet begins half-century of teaching and promoting good causes in Philadelphia

James Oglethorpe advances a number of reasons, some philanthropic, to show why a colony should be planted in Georgia

1737   Jean Louis makes gift for founding Charity Hospital, New Orleans

1739–41   George Whitefield, on second visit to America, finds religious revivals in progress and helps turn them into Great Awakening; founds orphanage in Georgia in 1740

1751–52   Dr. Thomas Bond, assisted by Benjamin Franklin and others, founds Pennsylvania Hospital, the first general hospital in the U.S.; building opened 1756

1760   New York, Virginia, Maryland, Pennsylvania, New Hampshire, and Rhode Island collect and send assistance to Boston fire sufferers

1767   Philadelphia Bettering House, sometimes called "Pauper Palace" opened

1774–75   Parliamentary act closing Boston Port creates greatest relief problem in colonial period; other towns and colonies send money, grain, and livestock to aid Boston

1776   Society for Alleviating the Miseries of Public Prisons, earliest prison reform society, organized in Philadelphia; reactivated in 1787

1780   Pennsylvania, first state to take such action, passes Act for the Gradual Abolition of Slavery

1790   Free mulattoes of Charleston, S.C., organize Brown Fellowship Society, one of several aristocratic charitable associations of that city

Death of Benjamin Franklin; will establishes Franklin Funds in Boston and Philadelphia to lend money to "young married artificers of good character"

1793   Yellow-fever epidemic in Philadelphia; worst disaster of kind in American history

1808   Andover Theological Seminary founded; popular cause among orthodox Congregational donors

1809   Mother Elizabeth Bayley Seton establishes order of Sisters of Charity of St. Joseph at Emmitsburg, Md.

1810   American Board of Commissioners for Foreign Missions organized; sends first missionaries to India in 1812

1811   Massachusetts General Hospital, favorite beneficiary of Boston philanthropists, founded

1816   American Bible Society, oldest of national benevolent societies, established; American Tract Society (1825), American Society for Promotion of Temperance (1826), and similar organizations founded in 1820's

1817   Thomas Hopkins Gallaudet (1787–1851) establishes in Hartford, Conn., America's first free school for deaf; one son to continue active in education of deaf until 1917

1818   Postwar depression prompts establishment of New York Society for the Prevention of Pauperism; similar societies in Baltimore and Philadelphia

1819   Supreme Court decision in Dartmouth College Case strengthens legal position of incorporated endowments

1821   Amherst College opens and receives liberal support from conservative Congregationalists

1824   Louis Dwight founds Boston Prison Discipline Society; controversy over relative merits of "Congregate" and "Separate" prison systems

1824–30   Samuel Gridley Howe takes part in, raises funds for, and administers relief in Greek War for Independence

1825   Founding of New York House of Refuge, first reformatory for juveniles; similar institutions in Boston and Philadelphia

Robert Owen (1771–1858) opens co-operative community in New Harmony, Ind.

American Philanthropy

1825–30   Boston Unitarians support Joseph Tuckerman's ministry to the poor

1829   Mathew Carey (1760–1839) attempts federated fundraising in Philadelphia

1831   Arthur (1786–1865) and Lewis Tappan (1788–1873), New York dry goods merchants, become active in antislavery and manual-training college movements

Death of Stephen Girard; left largest fortune any American had thus far accumulated to charitable purposes

Amos Lawrence (1786–1852) retires from business to devote full time to benevolent interests and spiritual welfare

1832   Samuel Gridley Howe opens New England Asylum (later Perkins Institution), leading American institution for instruction of the blind

1835   Alexis de Tocqueville comments on American disposition to organize and join voluntary associations in *Democracy in America*

1836   John Lowell bequeaths $250,000 to found and support Lowell Institute, Boston; annual lecture series begins in 1840

1837   Samuel G. Howe begins instruction of Laura Bridgman, blind and deaf girl

Horace Mann begins work as Secretary of Massachusetts Board of Education

Depression opens; lasts until 1840's

1841   Dorothea L. Dix (1802–87) begins crusade for better treatment of insane; submits *Memorial* to Massachusetts legislature in 1843; publishes *Remarks on Prisons and Prison Discipline*, 1845

1843   Robert Hartley and other charity reformers organize New York Association for Improving the Condition of the Poor

1845   Establishment of first American conference of Society of St. Vincent de Paul, charitable organization of Roman Catholic laymen

1846   After decade of debate Congress passes act creating Smithsonian Institution

1846–47   Large American contributions for Irish famine relief

Important Dates

1847   Abbott Lawrence makes gift of $50,000 to Harvard; gift helps support work of Louis Agassiz

1848   Girard College opens in Philadelphia; most famous orphanage in United States and classic example of the "dead hand" in philanthropy

1851   Y.M.C.A. movement spreads to the United States

1853   Charles Loring Brace founds Children's Aid Society of New York, important child welfare agency

1854   Congress passes, President Pierce vetoes, Dorothea Dix's bill granting public lands to states to assist in financing care of insane

1859   Peter Cooper (1791–1883), one of best-loved American philanthropists, opens Cooper Union in New York City as center for free instruction in art and science

1861   United States Sanitary Commission, forerunner of American Red Cross, organized

1862   Freedmen's aid societies established in North to send teachers and relief supplies to former slaves

1863   Massachusetts establishes first central agency for supervising public welfare institutions

           Catholic Protectory, largest institution for children in the United States, founded in New York City

1863–64 Sanitary Fairs in northern cities raise money and collect supplies for United States Sanitary Commission

1865   Freedmen's Bureau founded; active in relief and education in the South until early 1870's

1867   Peabody Fund, first of modern foundations, established by George Peabody (1795–1869) to assist southern education

1868   Opening of Hampton Institute in Hampton, Va.; best endowed school for Negroes

1869   Founding of London Charity Organization Society, which served as a model for American C.O.S. movement

1871–72 Fire sufferers in Chicago and Boston relieved by contributions from other cities

1874   Organization of National Conference of Charities and Correction, now National Conference on Social Welfare

1876   Opening of Jubilee Hall, Fisk University, Nashville,

Tenn.; money raised by concert tours of Fisk Jubilee Singers

1877 Buffalo Charity Organization Society established; similar organizations founded in other cities in next few years

1881 Clara Barton (1821–1912) organizes American Association of the Red Cross (name changed to American National Red Cross in 1893)

Booker T. Washington (1858–1915) organizes Tuskegee Institute for Negroes in Tuskegee, Ala.

1882 United States ratifies Geneva Convention of 1864, which provided for neutralization of aid to wounded in time of war

John F. Slater Fund founded to support Negro industrial schools and teacher training institutions

1884 Toynbee Hall, first social settlement, opened in London; visited by many Americans and served as model for American settlement houses

Hebrew Sheltering and Immigrant Aid Society organized to receive and assist Jews emigrating to the U.S.

1885 Stanford University chartered (opened 1891); gifts of Leland Stanford thought to be of unprecedented size

1887 Helen Keller (1880——), blind and deaf, begins study with Anne Sullivan

1888 Denver experiments with federated fund raising

1889 Andrew Carnegie publishes "Wealth"

John D. Rockefeller gives $600,000 to help found new University of Chicago

Jane Addams (1860–1935) establishes Hull House

1891 Rockefeller employs Frederick T. Gates as assistant in charitable matters

1892 New York *Tribune* counts 4,047 millionaires in the United States

1895 Washington Gladden publishes article on "tainted money"

Jewish Charities in Boston adopt federated fund-raising

1898 New York School of Philanthropy inaugurates formal training courses for social work

1899 First American Juvenile Court established in Chicago

1900 American National Red Cross obtains charter of incorporation from Congress

1901 Rockefeller Institute for Medical Research incorporated and begins work on small scale; eventually received $60.5 million from Rockefeller

1902 General Education Board established by John D. Rockefeller; his total gifts to it were about $130 million; Board in process of liquidation in late 1950's

Carnegie endows Carnegie Institution of Washington to encourage investigation, research, and discovery

1904 National Tuberculosis Association organized

1905 Carnegie Foundation for the Advancement of Teaching established

Resumption of tainted-money controversy

1907 Russell Sage Foundation, important in development of social work, organized

1909 First White House Conference on the Care of Dependent Children recommends establishment of federal Children's Bureau and declares that poverty alone should not be grounds for removing children from families

1910 Boy Scouts of America founded (Campfire Girls, 1910; Girl Scouts, 1912)

1911 Carnegie Corporation, Carnegie's largest foundation ($125 million), established

Missouri and Illinois enact "mothers' pensions" laws permitting assistance from public funds to maintain small children in own homes

1912 Congress establishes U.S. Children's Bureau "to investigate and report upon all matters pertaining to the welfare of children and child life among all classes of our people"

1913 Rockefeller Foundation chartered by State of New York "to promote the well-being of mankind throughout the world"

American Cancer Association founded

Modern community chest movement begins in Cleveland

1914 Red Cross "Mercy Ship" takes doctors, nurses, and hospital equipment to Europe at start of war

Commission for Relief in Belgium organized

American Jewish Joint Distribution Committee organized to co-ordinate Jewish war relief activities

Cleveland Foundation, first community trust, established

American Philanthropy

1915–16   U.S. Industrial Relations Commission investigates foundations

1917   Julius Rosenwald Fund established; active in field of Negro education

Income tax law permits individuals to deduct charitable contributions up to 15 per cent of taxable income

Publication of Mary Richmond's *Social Diagnosis*, landmark in social work

American Friends Service Committee begins operations

Red Cross asks—and gets—$100 million, largest sum raised by voluntary organizations up to that time

1918   Harkness family establishes Commonwealth Fund "to do something for the welfare of mankind"; active mainly in health field

United War Work campaign raises $200 million for seven national war relief agencies

Bequest of John W. Sterling doubles Yale's endowment

1919   Death of Andrew Carnegie, benefactions total $350 million

Harvard uses professional fund-raising counsel in $14 million endowment fund drive

Community chest in about 40 cities; spreads to 350 in 1929

Herbert Hoover (1874——) director of American Relief Administration; also Director General of Relief for Allied Governments

Twentieth Century Fund established by Edward A. Filene; specializes in economic research

1921   American Foundation for Blind founded; Helen Keller helps raise endowment

1921–22   Russian famine relief supervised by American Relief Administration, private organization headed by Herbert Hoover

1924   Total annual charitable contributions in United States reach $2 billion

1925   John Simon Guggenheim Memorial Foundation organized to aid young scholars and creative workers

1927   Restoration of Williamsburg, Va., financed by John D. Rockefeller, Jr. (1874——), begins

1928   Philanthropic peak of 1920's; 500 Lump-sum gifts of $1 million or more

Important Dates

Edward S. Harkness (1874–1940) gives $11 million to Harvard for house plan

1930 Kellogg Foundation organized; interested in health and education in rural areas

Louis Bamberger and Mrs. Felix Fuld donate $8 million to found Institute for Advanced Study, Princeton, N.J.

Edward S. Harkness makes large gifts to Yale and Phillips Exeter Academy

1931 Red Cross refuses to consider congressional grant for drought relief

President's Organization for Unemployment Relief conducts publicity campaign for local fund appeals

As a "temporary emergency" New York State assists local communities in financing unemployment relief

1932 Dedication of Folger Shakespeare Library, Washington, D.C., gift of Henry C. Folger

Red Cross processes and distributes surplus wheat and cotton to needy

Reconstruction Finance Corporation authorized to lend money to states for unemployment relief

FERA established to make emergency grants for unemployment relief

1933 Philanthropy at depression low point

Henry Ford opens Ford Museum and Greenfield Village

Rockefeller Foundation appropriates $1.5 million to expedite discovery of remedies for the depression

1934 First President's Birthday Ball for relief of polio victims

1935 Social Security Act, beginning of a permanent welfare program by national government

Heavier income and corporation taxes; corporations permitted to deduct charitable contributions up to 5 per cent of taxable income

Total contributions to philanthropy slightly exceed predepression peak

1936 Ford Foundation organized; not active nationally until about 1950

1937 Congress accepts Andrew Mellon's offer to give art collection and National Gallery building to public

Death of John D. Rockefeller; benefactions total $530 million

American Philanthropy

1938   National Foundation for Infantile Paralysis begins concentrated program of research into the cause, prevention, and treatment of poliomyelitis

1939   Neutrality Act requires agencies engaged in relief activities in belligerent countries to register with Department of State

1941   Red Cross adopts blood-donor program
    U.S.O. organized

1942   National War Fund, Inc., organized to collect funds for both war- and non-war agencies

1943   United Nations Relief and Rehabilitation Administration (UNRRA) founded to plan and supervise postwar emergency relief on international basis
    American Council of Voluntary Agencies for Foreign Service established by approximately fifty agencies to plan and co-ordinate private efforts

1945   CARE begins sending food parcels to Europe

1946   Voluntary agencies begin sending aid to Germany
    War Relief Control Board succeeded by Advisory Committee on Foreign Aid
    John D. Rockefeller, Jr., gives seventeen acres of downtown Manhattan land as site for United Nations headquarters
    Congress passes Full Employment Act, recognition of government's continuing responsibility to promote economic security

1946–48   United Jewish Appeal raises very large sums to assist refugees, immigrants to Israel, and government of Israel

1948   Senator Charles Tobey investigates use of foundations by business firms for non-philanthropic purposes

1949   President Truman announces Point 4 plan of technical assistance to underdeveloped nations
    United Fund movement begins in Detroit

1950   Revision of Internal Revenue Code subjects foundations engaged in certain prohibited practices to loss of tax exemption

1951   U.S.O. reactivated

1952   Select (Cox) Committee of House of Representatives investigates foundations

Important Dates

1953   Carnegie Endowment for International Peace opens International Center on United Nations Plaza, New York

Decision of New Jersey Supreme Court in *Barlow et al. v. A. P. Smith Manufacturing Co.* clarifies legal right of corporations to make contributions to higher education

1954   Special (Reece) Committee of House of Representatives widely criticized for tactics employed in investigation of foundations

1955   Ford Foundation announces largest grant in foundation history: $560 million to privately supported colleges, medical schools, and hospitals

National Merit Scholarship Corporation organized to assist talented students attend colleges of their choice

Development of Salk vaccine against paralytic polio climaxes seventeen years of work by National Foundation for Infantile Paralysis

1958   National Foundation for Infantile Paralysis becomes National Foundation; will combat rheumatic diseases, birth defects, and disorders of central nervous system

1959   Disc jockey Peter Tripp stays awake longer than anyone in history: performs for 200 hours without sleep (in Armed Forces recruiting booth, Times Square) "in the interest of science and the March of Dimes"

Suggested Reading

GENERAL

Although a great deal has been written on topics falling within the range of philanthropy, American historians have only recently begun to regard philanthropy itself as an interesting and profitable subject of research. The logical starting place for advanced students is the Russell Sage Foundation's *Report of the Princeton Conference on the History of Philanthropy in the United States* (1956), which suggests areas needing to be explored and contains a useful annotated bibliography prepared by Margaret M. Otto in consultation with F. Emerson Andrews. Merle Curti, in his article "The History of American Philanthropy as a Field of Research," *American Historical Review*, LXII (January, 1957), 352–63, assays past research in the field and also points out new paths of inquiry.

The standard encyclopedias include useful articles on charity or philanthropy. C. S. Loch's "Charity and Charities," *Encyclopaedia Brittanica*, V (11th ed., 1910), 860–91, is a classic; and Kenneth L. M. Pray's "Charity," *Encyclopedia of the Social Sciences*, III (1930), 340–45, and Edward Grubb's "Philanthropy," *Encyclopedia of Religion and Ethics*, IX (1928), 837–40, deserve notice. The index volumes of both the *Dictionary of American Biography* (1928–37) and *National Cyclopaedia of American Biography* (1893——) list subjects of biographies by occupation and happily include "Philanthropist" as an occupation. W. D. P. Bliss (ed.), *The New*

Suggested Reading

Encyclopedia of Social Reform (1908) covers a broad range of topics and is still helpful. For contemporary welfare problems, the best reference work is Russell Kurtz (ed.), *Social Work Yearbook* (1957, new ed., 1960). The *Yearbook* contains an excellent concise history of "The Development of Social Welfare Programs in the United States" by H. L. Lurie, articles ranging from "Administration of Social Agencies" to "Youth Services"—many with historical sections and all with bibliographies and a comprehensive directory of international, national, and voluntary welfare agencies.

F. Emerson Andrews', *Philanthropic Giving* (1950), an informed, witty, and sensible book is the best introduction to the complexities and technicalities of philanthropy. Walter A. Friedlander's *An Introduction to Social Welfare* (1955) is a superior textbook with helpful bibliographical suggestions. Nathan E. Cohen, in *Social Work in the American Tradition* (1958), relates trends in the profession of social work to general historical developments. Henry Winfred Thurston's *The Dependent Child* (1930) surveys methods of foster care of children in England and the United States. Public efforts in relief and welfare from the colonial period through the New Deal are traced in Arthur P. Miles's *An Introduction to Public Welfare* (1950). Sophonisba P. Breckinridge's *Public Welfare Administration* (1938) and Edith Abbott's *Public Assistance* (1940) are collections of documents with helpful introductions and, in the latter book, papers on the incongruities of the American poor law system.

Merle Curti's "American Philanthropy and the National Character," *American Quarterly*, X (Winter 1958), 420–37, provides a great deal of information on American attitudes toward philanthropy. Professor Curti is now preparing a history of American overseas aid. Edward C. Jenkins' *Philanthropy in America* (1950) deals mainly with the organization and financing of philanthropic agencies in the twentieth century but also gives some attention to the role of philanthropy in American life. Two studies by professional fund-raisers, Arnaud C. Marts, *Philanthropy's Role in Civilization: Its Contribution to Human Freedom* (1953), and John Price Jones, *The American Giver: A Review of American Generosity* (1954), offer practical and inspirational insights into the business of giving. Irvin G. Wyllie, in "The Reputation of the American Philanthropist," *Social Service Review*, XXXII (1958),

American Philanthropy

215–22, examines public reaction to philanthropic gifts. Professor Wyllie is currently studying the ideology of American philanthropy. Ralph E. Pumphrey's "Compassion and Protection: Dual Motives in Social Welfare," *Social Service Review*, XXXIII (1959) 21–29, analyzes two broad themes in philanthropy.

Lynn Thorndike's "The Historical Background" in Ellsworth Faris *et al.* (eds.), *Intelligent Philanthropy* (1930) sketches ancient and medieval antecedents of modern charity and poor relief. W. K. Jordan's *Philanthropy in England, 1480–1660* (1959) is the most important and authoritative work on the English background of modern philanthropy. Professor David Owen is completing a study of English philanthropy in the Victorian period. Two older books by B. Kirkman Gray, *A History of English Philanthropy* (1905) and *Philanthropy and the State* (1908), contain thoughtful passages on the uses and limitations of philanthropy. Karl de Schweinitz' *England's Road to Social Security* (1943) is a stimulating book by a leading American social worker. Sir William H. Beveridge's *Voluntary Action: A Report on Methods of Social Advance* (1948) is a warm tribute to philanthropic activity by one of the greatest advocates of the twentieth-century welfare state.

CHAPTER I

The writings of John Winthrop, William Penn, and Cotton Mather are primary sources for philanthropic thought in the early colonial period. Winthrop's "A Model of Christian Charity" (1630) is available in the Massachusetts Historical Society's, *Winthrop Papers*, II (1931), 282–95, and in abridged form in Perry Miller (ed.), *The American Puritans: Their Prose and Poetry* (1956). Samuel Eliot Morison's *Builders of the Bay Colony* (1930) has a good chapter on Winthrop; the best recent study is by Edmund S. Morgan, *The Puritan Dilemma: The Story of John Winthrop* (1958). Frederick B. Tolles and E. Gordon Aldefer (eds.), in their *The Witness of William Penn* (1957), provide selections from *No Cross, No Crown* (1669, 1682, 1694), *Some Fruits of Solitude* (1693), and *More Fruits of Solitude* (1702). Edward Beatty's *William Penn as Social Philosopher* (1939) and Auguste Jorns's *The Quakers as Pioneers in Social Work* (1931) are standard interpretations of Quaker humanitarianism. Cotton Mather's *Bonifacius, or Essays To*

Suggested Reading

Do Good (1710, often reprinted) is required reading. *Magnalia Christi Americana* (1855 ed.), I, 102, contains Mather's advice to Bostonians on the conduct of charity. Kenneth B. Murdock's introduction to his *Selections from Cotton Mather* (1926) helped revive respect for Mather; Perry Miller's *The New England Mind: From Colony to Province* (1953) offers the most learned recent analysis of Mather's thought. Elizabeth Wisner, in her article on "The Puritan Background of the New England Poor Laws," *Social Service Review*, XIX (1945), 381–90, examines Mather's charitable activities from the standpoint of modern social work.

Among Benjamin Franklin's numerous essays on charity and poor relief the following are especially interesting: "On the Price of Corn, and Management of the Poor" (1766), "On the Laboring Poor" (1768), and "On the Institution in Holland to Prevent Poverty" (1772). These are all in Albert Henry Smyth (ed.), *The Writings of Benjamin Franklin* (1907), as are Franklin's *Autobiography* and *The Way to Wealth*. Carl Van Doren's *Benjamin Franklin's Autobiographical Writings* (1945) is a handy anthology; and the best brief biography is Carl L. Becker's "Benjamin Franklin," in the *Dictionary of American Biography*, VI (1931), 585–98. Bradford Smith's *A Dangerous Freedom* (1952) is one of several works which comment on Franklin's use of voluntary associations.

Marcus W. Jernegan's pioneering work, *Laboring and Dependent Classes in Colonial America, 1607–1783* (1931), contains chapters on poor relief in Virginia and New England. The problems of urban poverty and its treatment are well covered in Carl Bridenbaugh's *Cities in the Wilderness: The First Century of Urban Life in America, 1625–1742* (1938) and *Cities in Revolt: Urban Life in America, 1743–1776* (1955). Both Robert W. Kelso's *The History of Public Relief in Massachusetts, 1620–1920* (1922) and David M. Schneider's *History of Public Welfare in New York, 1609–1866* (1938) are particularly useful for the colonial period. Verner W. Crane's *The Southern Frontier, 1670–1732* (1929) and Daniel J. Boorstin's *The Americans: The Colonial Experience* (1958) deal with the philanthropic motive in the founding of Georgia. The latter attributes the failure of the project, in part, to philanthropy's want of an experimental spirit.

CHAPTER II

Ola Elizabeth Winslow's *Jonathan Edwards, 1703–1758* (1940) and William Warren Sweet's *Religion in Colonial America* (1942) draw attention to the social results of the Great Awakening. Stow Persons' *American Minds* (1958) dissents from the view that the Awakening subsided rapidly after 1742. Stuart C. Henry's *George Whitefield, Wayfaring Witness* (1957) is the most recent biography of the English evangelist. Although mainly concerned with English developments, Eric McCoy North, in his *Early Methodist Philanthropy* (1914), includes material on Whitefield's orphan house in Georgia. James Dow McCallum, in *Eleazar Wheelock, Founder of Dartmouth College* (1939) and a compilation of *The Letters of Wheelock's Indians* (1932), records the various trials of another colonial philanthropic enterprise. William L. Sachse's *The Colonial American in Britain* (1956) contains data on attempts of colonial colleges to raise funds abroad.

George S. Brookes's *Friend Anthony Benezet* (1937), a loving biography, includes letters to, from, and concerning Benezet and Benezet's minor writings. Anthony Benezet's *Some Observations on the Situation, Disposition, and Character of the Indian Natives of the Continent* (1784) is characteristic of the author. *A Word of Remembrance and Caution to the Rich* (1793), written about thirty years before publication and originally entitled "A Plea for the Poor," is John Woolman's best essay. Frederick B. Tolles's *Meeting House and Counting House* (1948) gives an excellent picture of the Quaker society in which Benezet and Woolman lived.

Carl and Jessica Bridenbaugh, in *Rebels and Gentlemen: Philadelphia in the Age of Franklin* (1942) discuss the Pennsylvania Hospital and other benevolent institutions. Richard H. Shryock's *The Development of Modern Medicine* (1936) relates medical developments to humanitarian movements and shows the relationship between European and American activity. This relationship is the subject of Michael Kraus's "Eighteenth Century Humanitarianism: Collaboration between Europe and America," *Pennsylvania Magazine of History and Biography*, LX (1936), 270–86. Merrill Jensen's *The New Nation* (1950) has a chapter surveying humanitarian progress during the Confederation period. Benjamin Rush's *Essays, Literary, and Philosophical* (1806) is a fascinating miscellany by

Suggested Reading

one of America's greatest humanitarian reformers. George W. Corner's edition of *The Autobiography of Benjamin Rush* (1948) is valuable and L. H. Butterfield's *Letters of Benjamin Rush* (1951) is priceless. John Harvey Powell, in *Bring Out Your Dead* (1949), deals with Philadelphia's reaction to the yellow-fever epidemic of 1793 in a manner both vivid and scholarly. John Bach McMaster, in *The Life and Times of Stephen Girard* (1918), makes Girard's career dull; Harry Emerson Wildes's *Lonely Midas: The Story of Stephen Girard* (1943) overcompensates for McMaster's defects but is more satisfactory. Neva R. Deardorff's "The New Pied Pipers," *Survey*, LII (1924), 31–47, 56–61, comments on Girard's legacy and its influence on other donors.

CHAPTERS III AND IV

Two volumes in the "History of American Life" series, John A. Krout and Dixon Ryan Fox, *The Completion of Independence, 1790–1830* (1944) and Carl Russell Fish, *The Rise of the Common Man, 1830–1850* (1927), provide the social background for philanthropic developments in the first half of the nineteenth century. John Bach McMaster's *A History of the People of the United States*, IV (1895) and V (1900), and Edward Channing's *A History of the United States*, V (1922), give more space to philanthropy than do most of the general histories. The fullest treatment is in Emerson Davis' *The Half Century* (1851). *Niles' Register* (1811–49), which is indexed, contains a surprising amount of material on poor relief. Nearly all European travelers' accounts, including those of Tocqueville and Dickens, devote space to American philanthropic institutions. One of the lesser known but valuable accounts is George Combe's *Notes on the United States of North America* (1841). George Wilson Pierson's *Tocqueville and Beaumont in America* (1938) presents a panorama of the United States in 1831–32.

Edith Abbott's *Some American Pioneers in Social Welfare* (1937) contains biographical sketches and selections from the writings of Thomas Eddy, Stephen Girard, Samuel Gridley Howe, Dorothea L. Dix, and Charles Loring Brace. Joseph Tuckerman, *On the Elevation of Poor* (1874) reprints selections from Tuckerman's reports on his ministry to the poor in Boston. Mathew Carey's proposal for federated financing in Philadelphia in 1829 is reprinted in the *Social Service Review*, XXIX (1955), 302–5. *The Works of William E. Channing, D.D.* (1887) includes "Remarks on Associations" and other relevant essays and addresses. William R. Lawrence's *Extracts from the Diary and Correspondence of the Late Amos Lawrence* (1855) is illuminating; and Lewis Tappan's *Is It Right To Be Rich?* (1869) follows in the pattern of Mather's *Essays To Do Good.* Both Emerson and Thoreau made pointed observations on philanthropy in their journals and essays. "Self-Reliance" (1836–39), "Man the Reformer" (1841), and "New England Reformers" (1844) give Emerson's views. *Walden* (1854) is salted with Thoreau's peppery comments.

Franklin Parker's "George Peabody, Founder of Modern Philanthropy" (Ph.D. diss., Peabody College, 1956) is a detailed study of an important figure. Helen E. Marshall's *Dorothea Dix, Forgotten Samaritan* (1937) and Harold Schwartz's *Samuel Gridley Howe, Social Reformer* (1956) are both excellent. Many of the philanthropists and reformers of the middle period still await their biographers, but Daniel T. McColgan's *Joseph Tuckerman* (1940), Benjamin P. Thomas' *Theodore Weld* (1950), and R. V. Harlow's *Gerrit Smith, Philanthropist and Reformer* (1939) do their subjects justice.

A number of topical studies are particularly useful for the pre-Civil War reforms: Albert Deutsch, *The Mentally Ill in America* (1949); Blake McKelvey, *American Prisons* (1936); Merle Curti, *The Social Ideas of American Educators* (1935) and *Peace or War* (1936); Ishbel Ross, *Journey into Light: The Story of the Education of the Blind* (1951); Harry Best, *Blindness and the Blind in the United States* (1934) and *Deafness and the Deaf in the United States* (1943). More specialized studies include: John R. Bodo, *The Protestant Clergy and Public Issues, 1812–1848* (1954); Clifford S. Griffin, "Religious Benevolence as Social Control, 1815–60," *Mississippi Valley Historical Review*, XLIV (1957–58), 423–44; and Irwin G. Wyllie, "The Search for An American Law of Charity" *Mississippi Valley Historical Review*, XLVI (1959), 203–21. Gilbert Hobbs Barnes's *The Anti-Slavery Impulse, 1830–1844* (1933), Henrietta Buckmaster's *Let My People Go* (1941), and William H. Siebert's *The Underground Railroad from Slavery to Freedom* (1898) are convenient sources for philanthropic participation in the antislavery movement. The work of Charles Loring Brace is

Suggested Reading

discussed in Thurston's *The Dependent Child,* pp. 92–131; Brace's own book, *The Dangerous Classes of New York and Twenty Years' Work among Them* (1872), is a fascinating account of "child saving."

CHAPTER V

The chapter on charity in Emerson David Fite's *Social and Industrial Conditions in the North during the Civil War* (1910) is still useful; Ellis Merton Coulter, in *The Confederate States of America, 1861–65* (1950), throws light on war relief in the South. There is a wealth of material on charitable fairs and Lincoln's support of them in Carl Sandburg's *Abraham Lincoln: The War Years* (1939). William Quentin Maxwell's *Lincoln's Fifth Wheel: The Political History of the United States Sanitary Commission* (1956) is admirable; George Worthington Adams' *Doctors in Blue: The Medical History of the Union Army in the Civil War* (1952) offers additional information on the working of the Sanitary Commission. George R. Bentley's *A History of the Freedmen's Bureau* (1955), the latest full-length study, can be usefully supplemented by John and La Wanda Cox's "General O. O. Howard and the 'Misrepresented Bureau,' " *Journal of Southern History,* XIX (1953), 427–56. The best treatment of the freedmen's aid societies is in Henry Lee Swint's *The Northern Teacher in the South, 1862–1870* (1941).

CHAPTER VI

Allan Nevins' *Emergence of Modern America* (1927) and Arthur M. Schlesinger's *Rise of the City* (1933) have proved their worth to a generation of students. Howard D. Kramer has two helpful articles on a somewhat neglected topic: "The Beginning of the Public Health Movement in the United States," *Bulletin of the History of Medicine,* XXI (1947), 352–76; and "Effect of the Civil War on the Public Health Movement," *Mississippi Valley Historical Review,* XXXV (1948), 449–62. Two studies of unusual value are Leah H. Feder, *Unemployment Relief in Periods of Depression* (1936), which covers the years 1857–1922, and Emma O. Lundberg, *Unto the Least of These* (1947), a history of social services for children.

Frank D. Watson's *The Charity Organization Movement in the*

United States (1922) is still the standard work in its field, but a new study by Verl S. Lewis is in progress. The best study of the origin and development of the family service movement is Margaret E. Rich's *A Belief in People: A History of Family Social Work* (1956). Amos G. Warner's *American Charities* (1894) is indispensable for an understanding of the point of view of charity reformers in the late nineteenth century. Robert H. Bremner, in " 'Scientific Philanthropy,' 1873–93," *Social Service Review*, XXX (June, 1956), 168–73, gives citations to the voluminous contemporary literature on the subject. There are interesting comments on the "new charity" in Samuel Rezneck's "Patterns of Thought and Action in an American Depression, 1882–1886," *American Historical Review*, LXI (1955–56), 284–307. Jane Addams *et al.*, *Philanthropy and Social Progress* (1893), present the attitude of more advanced social workers in the 1890's. William Rhinelander Stewart's *The Philanthropic Work of Josephine Shaw Lowell* (1911) is still the only full-length study of one of the most important women of the late nineteenth century. Frances A. Goodale's anthology, *The Literature of Philanthropy* (1893), describes in winning fashion the work of women volunteers in many undertakings.

Boris D. Bogen's *Jewish Philanthropy* (1917) is still a valuable reference. A more recent survey is Herman D. Stein's "Jewish Social Work in the United States (1654–1954)," *American Jewish Year Book*, LVII (1956), 3–98. Barbara Miller Solomon, in *Pioneers in Service* (1956), provides a detailed study of the organization and work of the Associated Jewish Philanthropies of Boston. John O'Grady's *Catholic Charities in the United States* (1931) is comprehensive and authoritative. Daniel T. McColgan, in *A Century of Charity* (1951), records the history of the Society of St. Vincent de Paul in the United States. Both Charles Hopkins' *History of the Y.M.C.A. in North America* (1951) and Foster Rhea Dulles' *The American Red Cross* (1950) are readable and objective. The newest and most acceptable biography of Clara Barton is *Angel of the Battlefield* (1956) by Ishbel Ross.

CHAPTER VII

Andrew Carnegie's "Wealth," *North American Review*, CXLVIII (1889), 653–64, and "Best Fields for Philanthropy," *North American Review*, CXLIX (1889), 682–98, are reprinted in his *The Gospel*

Suggested Reading

of *Wealth* (1901). Burton J. Hendrick, in *The Life of Andrew Carnegie* (1932) sketches the background and reception of the gospel of wealth and gives some information on Carnegie's major gifts. Carnegie's benefactions are summarized by Robert M. Lester in *Forty Years of Carnegie Giving* (1941). John D. Rockefeller, in *Random Reminiscences of Men and Events* (1909), states his philosophy and program for giving. Allan Nevins' *Study in Power: John D. Rockefeller, Industrialist and Philanthropist* (1953) describes the difficulties Rockefeller encountered in carrying out his stewardship. *American Heritage,* VI (April, 1955), 65–86, contains the memoirs of Frederick T. Gates, Rockefeller's adviser on philanthropy, with an introduction and postscript by Allan Nevins. Raymond B. Fosdick's *John D. Rockefeller, Jr.* (1956), one of the most distinguished biographies of recent years, shows the broadening influence exerted on the younger Rockefeller by Gates and others with whom he was associated in managing the family benefactions.

Albert Shaw, in "American Millionaires and Their Public Gifts," *Review of Reviews,* VII (1893), 48–60, surveys the extent to which the gospel of wealth was being practiced by millionaires in the 1890's. Sarah K. Bolton's *Famous Givers and Their Gifts* (1896) deals with several almost forgotten donors as well as with many well-known ones. Edward C. Kirkland's *Dream and Thought in the Business Community, 1860–1900* (1956) and Irvin G. Wyllie's *The Self-Made Man in America* (1954) are useful on businessmen's attitudes toward philanthropy. Washington Gladden, with his article "Tainted Money," *Outlook,* LII (1895), 886–87, opened a celebrated controversy. E. Franklin Frazier's *Black Bourgeoisie* (1957) and Louis R. Harlan's *Separate and Unequal: Public School Campaigns and Racism in the Southern Seaboard States, 1901–1915* (1958) are critical of the influence of northern philanthropists on Negro education; Horace Mann Bond, *The Education of the Negro in the American Social Order* (1934) is a balanced account. Gunnar Myrdal *et al.,* in *An American Dilemma* (1944), II, 887–93, offer a quick survey of philanthropic activity in the field of southern education.

In *When Social Work was Young* (1939) Edward T. Devine records the variety of causes in which social workers were active around and after the turn of the century. The anti-tuberculosis crusade, which touched on many other issues, is treated in Richard H. Shryock's *National Tuberculosis Association (1904–1954)* (1957).

American Philanthropy

Robert H. Bremner, in *From the Depths: The Discovery of Poverty in the United States* (1956), discusses the role of social workers in reform movements of the Progressive era. Jane Addams' *Democracy and Social Ethics* (1902) and *Twenty Years at Hull-House* (1910) illumine the practical idealism of the settlement movement. Another settlement leader is memorialized in R. L. Duffus' *Lillian Wald* (1938). Florence Kelley's "Labor Legislation and Philanthropy in Illinois," *Charities Review*, X (1900–1901), 287–88, is a characteristic article by a formidable reformer. Her biographer is Josephine Goldmark, *Impatient Crusader: Florence Kelley's Life Story* (1953).

The Long View (1930) brings together some of the writings of Mary E. Richmond, an important figure in the development of social work. Miss Richmond's *Social Diagnosis* (1917), a description of the casework process, is one of the classics of social work. A biography of Miss Richmond by Muriel Pumphrey is forthcoming. Ernest V. Hollis' and Alice L. Taylor's *Social Work Education in the United States* (1951) contains a chapter on the history of schools of social work.

CHAPTER VIII

Dulles, *American Red Cross*, and Hopkins, *Y.M.C.A.*, are essential for war relief activities in World War I. Portia B. Kernodle's *The Red Cross Nurse in Action, 1882–1948* (1949) is thorough and unsentimental. Raymond B. Fosdick, in *Chronicle of a Generation: An Autobiography* (1958), describes the confusion resulting from the desire of numerous private agencies to serve the soldier. Frank M. Surface and Raymond L. Bland's *American Food in the World War and Reconstruction Period* (1931) is a methodical account of relief operations directed by Herbert Hoover in the decade after 1914. Two studies deal with special phases of Hoover's work: Suda L. Bane and Ralph H. Lutz, *Organization of American Relief in Europe, 1918–1919* (1943), and H. H. Fisher, *The Famine in Soviet Russia, 1919–1923: The Operations of the American Relief Administration* (1927). Frank Alfred Golder and Lincoln Hutchinson, in *On the Trail of the Russian Famine* (1927), report the observations of two A.R.A. investigators. Hoover's *An American Epic* (1959——), a "history of American enterprises of compassion," begins with a volume on the C.R.B.

John R. Seeley *et al.*, in *Community Chest: A Case Study in Phi-*

Suggested Reading

lanthropy (1958) focus on Indianapolis but present the historical background and development of the community chest movement. Willford Isbell King's *Trends in Philanthropy* (1928) studies patterns in giving in New Haven, 1900–1925. Henry S. Pritchett's "A Science of Giving," in Carnegie Corporation of New York, *Report of the Acting President* (1922), pp. 13–20, is a foundation executive's presentation of the difficulties of giving. A foundation founder discusses the same problem in Julius Rosenwald, "The Burden of Wealth," *Saturday Evening Post*, January 5, 1929, pp. 12–13. Cornelia Cannon's "Philanthropic Doubts," *Atlantic Monthly*, CXXVIII (1921), 289–300, critical of the philanthropic approach to social problems, received wide attention in the 1920's. "Giving—the Great American Game," *Saturday Evening Post*, December 28, 1928, p. 28, and "The New Gospel of Wealth," *Literary Digest*, November 30, 1929, pp. 22–23, are examples of the celebration of American philanthropy in the late 1920's.

CHAPTER IX

The availability of Arthur M. Schlesinger, Jr.'s *The Crisis of the Old Order, 1919–1933* (1957) makes it unnecessary to cite many works on the early depression years. Jonathan Leonard's *Three Years Down* (1939) preserves some of the flavor of the period. U.S. Senate Committee on Manufacture, 72 Congress, 1 session, *Unemployment Relief: Hearings on S. 174 . . . and S. 262* (1932), contains a mine of information. R. M. MacIver's *The Contributions of Sociology to Social Work* (1931), Reinhold Niebuhr's *The Contributions of Religion to Social Work* (1932), and Philip Klein's "Social Work," *Encyclopedia of the Social Sciences*, XIV (1935), 165–73, are all important sources for the orientation of social workers' thought in the early 1930's. Rich, *A Belief in People*, is particularly good on the impact of the depression on family welfare agencies. Abraham Epstein, in "Do the Rich Give to Charity?" *American Mercury*, XXIII (May, 1931), 22–30, discusses the inadequacy of philanthropy as a means of meeting social needs.

Harris G. Warren, in *Herbert Hoover and the Great Depression* (1959) attempts to do justice to the Hoover administration. The former President presents his own case in *The Memoirs of Herbert Hoover: The Great Depression, 1929–41* (1952). William Starr Myers' *The State Papers and Other Public Writings of Herbert*

Hoover (1934) is the standard source for Hoover's statements on charity and other subjects. Bernard Bellush, in *Franklin D. Roosevelt as Governor of New York* (1955), and Frank Freidel, in *Franklin D. Roosevelt: The Triumph* (1956), trace the development of Roosevelt's policy on unemployment relief. Dorothy Kahn's *This Business of Relief* (1936) is good on the situation in the mid-thirties. Josephine C. Brown's *Public Relief, 1929-1939* (1940) is the best guide to a complicated problem. Mabel Newcomer, in "Fifty Years of Public Support of Welfare Functions in the United States," *Social Service Review*, XV (1941), 651–60, records and comments on the changes in the financing of public welfare, 1890–1940. Marguerite T. Boylan's *Social Welfare in the Catholic Church* (1941) shows the impact of the depression and New Deal on organized Catholic charities.

CHAPTER X

There is an immense and growing literature on foundations. The best guide to it (and the best book on the subject) is F. Emerson Andrews' *Philanthropic Foundations* (1956). Wilmer Shields Rich, in *American Foundations and Their Fields* (1955) provides a comprehensive directory. Frederick P. Keppel's *The Foundation: Its Place in American Life* (1930) reflects the thoughtful and humane outlook of the author, who was president of the Carnegie Corporation. *Funds and Foundations* (1952), by Abraham Flexner, a foundation pioneer, is critical of foundation policies since the mid-1920's. There are histories of a number of the major foundations. The best is Raymond B. Fosdick's *The Story of the Rockefeller Foundation* (1952); the least reverent is Dwight Macdonald's *The Ford Foundation* (1956). Eduard C. Lindeman, in *Wealth and Culture* (1936), and Horace Coon, in *Money To Burn* (1938), emphasize the conservatism of the foundations. Joseph C. Kiger's *Operating Principles of the Larger Foundations* (1954) is a judicious study by the director of research for the Cox investigating committee. *Hearings before the Select (Cox) Committee to Investigate Tax-Exempt Foundations* (1953) is well worth consulting. Edwin R. Embree's "Timid Billions: Are the Foundations Doing Their Job?" *Harper's Magazine*, CXCVIII (March, 1949), 28–37, is the most challenging of the many articles criticizing the foundations in the late 1940's and early 1950's.

Suggested Reading

Other articles, too abundant to list here, are cited in *Report of the Princeton Conference.*

Joseph C. Hyman's *Twenty-Five Years of American Aid to Jews Overseas* (1939) is a modest and moving record of the work of the Joint Distribution Committee. David Hinshaw's *Rufus Jones, Master Quaker* (1951) contains material on the American Friends Service Committee in the 1920's and 30's. *Voluntary War Relief during World War II* (1946), a report by the U.S. President's War Relief Control Board, is a useful summary. A history of the National War Fund, *Design for Giving* (1947) by Harold J. Seymour is particularly good on fund-raising. George Woodbridge's *UNRRA: The History of the United Nations Relief and Rehabilitation Administration* (1950) is a distinguished official history. Edward McSweeney's *American Voluntary Aid to Germany, 1945–50* (1950) is a short summary. The Congressional (House) Special Subcommittee of the Committee on Foreign Affairs, in its *Final Report on Foreign Aid* (1948), concludes that Americans can afford to send private assistance overseas and cannot afford to discontinue it. Walter R. Sharp, in *International Technical Assistance* (1952), attempts to inventory and evaluate United States government, United Nations, and regional assistance programs. William Adams Brown, Jr., and Redvers Opie, in *American Foreign Assistance* (1953), appraise twelve years (1941–52) of overseas aid. The private agencies' tasks are explored by the American Council of Voluntary Agencies for Foreign Service in *The Role of Voluntary Agencies in Technical Assistance* (1953). Alvah Myrdal, Arthur J. Altmeyer, and Dean Rusk describe the challenge of *America's Role in International Social Welfare* (1955). Max F. Millikan and W. W. Rostow, in *A Proposal: Key to an Effective Foreign Policy* (1957) argue for expanded, long-term American participation in economic development of undeveloped areas. Grant S. McClellan's *United States Foreign Aid* (1957) presents arguments pro and con; and *Current History*, XXXIII (1957), 129–67, devotes an entire issue to an objective review of foreign-aid problems.

J. Frederic Dewhurst and Associates, in *America's Needs and Resources: A New Survey* (1955), pp. 430–68, describe the domestic welfare scene in the 1950's. Ida C. Meriam's "Social Welfare in the United States, 1934–54," *Social Security Bulletin*, XVIII (October,

1955), 3–14, presents developments since the New Deal. There are many helpful insights in Max Lerner's *America as a Civilization* (1957); the section entitled "The Sinews of Welfare," pp. 123–39, is particularly rewarding. Marion K. Sanders' "Mutiny of the Bountiful," *Harper's Magazine*, CCXVI (December, 1958), 23–31, deals with financing of voluntary health organizations. Wayne Mc-Millen, in "Financing Social Welfare Service," *Social Work Yearbook* (1957), pp. 260–67, discusses the United Fund movement, and in "Charitable Fraud: An Obstacle in Community Organization," *Social Service Review*, XXIX (1955), 153–71, he describes the more common charity rackets and examines their direct and indirect costs. The American Association of Fund-Raising Counsel's *Giving, U.S.A.* (1961) is a handy guide to the distribution of philanthropic giving. Harold L. Wilensky and Charles N. Lebeaux, in their *Industrial Society and Social Welfare* (1958), pp. 148–67, survey and analyze contemporary welfare programs and expenditures.

Acknowledgments

This study was supported in part by a grant-in-aid from the Ohio State University Research Foundation. It was written while I was associated with the History of American Philanthropy Project at the University of Wisconsin. I wish to express my appreciation to both institutions, and also to the staffs of the libraries of the Ohio State University, Wisconsin Historical Society, and University of Wisconsin. It was my good fortune to be able to discuss the work while it was in progress with Merle Curti and Irvin G. Wyllie of the University of Wisconsin. Mr. Curti and Mr. Wyllie have read the manuscript and have given me the benefit of their criticism, but they are not responsible for my interpretations, errors, or omissions. I also wish to thank Merle Rife and Richard Thomas, who helped me begin research for the book, and Mrs. Mildred Lloyd, who put the manuscript in shape for publication. Daniel J. Boorstin's suggestions have improved the readability of the book without altering its content or conclusions. Mrs. Catherine Marting Bremner made helpful comments on style, assisted in compiling the table of dates, and, like Sue and Ann Bremner, provided unfailing encouragement.

Index

Abolition movement, 50, 73–75
Acadians, 24, 27, 28
Act for International Development (1950), 181
Adams, John Quincy, 53
Addams, Jane, 192; and settlement movement, 113–15
Advisory Committee on Voluntary Aid, 182, 196
Africa, 48, 136, 182
Agassiz, Louis, 54, 191
Agricultural surpluses, 134, 152, 166, 183, 195
Agriculture, U.S. Department of, 119–20
Alcott, Louisa May, 78
Aldrich, Winthrop, 168
Almsgiving, 17, 108, 143, 186
Almshouse, 61–62, 96
American Aid to France, 169
American Anti-Slavery Society, 50
American Association for Labor Legislation, 123
American Association of the Red Cross, 93, 192. *See also* American National Red Cross
American Association for the Relief of Misery on the Battlefield, 92

American Association of Social Workers, 149
American Bible Society, 46, 79, 189
American Board of Commissioners for Foreign Missions, 189
American Cancer Society, 123, 180, 193
American Colonization Society, 48–49
American Committee for Armenian and Syrian Relief, 129
American Council of Learned Societies, 139
American Council of Voluntary Agencies for Foreign Service, 171, 182, 196
American Expeditionary Force, 131
American Foundation for the Blind, 156, 194
American Friends Service Committee, 135, 149, 166, 183, 194
American Heart Association, 180
American Jewish Joint Distribution Committee, 166, 173, 193
American Jewish Relief Committee, 129
American Medical Association, 44
American Mercury, 150

Index

American Missionary Association, 87, 88

American National Red Cross, 78, 82, 122, 128, 133, 135, 144, 149, 155, 166, 169, 192, 193, 194; blood donor program of, 167, 196; Christmas seal campaign of, 124; and disaster relief, 94; and distribution of surplus commodities (1932), 152, 195; drought relief program of (1931), 145, 195; founding of, 92–93; and fundraising in World War I, 130–31, 194; membership in, 125, 131; in Ohio-Mississippi floods (1937), 163; and War Council, 130; and war relief (1914–17), 125–29, 193; in World War I (1917–18), 129–32

American philanthropy. *See* Philanthropy

American Philosophical Society, 18

American Red Cross. *See* American National Red Cross

American Relief Administration, 134–35, 194. *See also* Russian famine relief

American Revolution, 23, 30, 31, 33–34, 36, 38

American Society for Promotion of Temperance, 46, 189

American Sunday School Union, 46

American Telephone and Telegraph Co., 146

American Tract Society, 79, 189

American Tuberculosis Association, 119, 123; Christmas seal campaign of, 124

Amherst College, 51, 52, 189

Andover Theological Seminary, 51, 66, 189

Appleton, Nathan, 49

Appleton, Samuel, 52

Appleton, William, 46

"Arbella" (ship), 7

ARK (American Relief for Korea), 171

Armenian massacres, 94

Asia, 182

Association for the Relief of Respectable Aged and Indigent Females, 46

Association of Community Chests and Councils, 145, 147

Associations, voluntary, 4, 7, 14, 18–19, 47, 114, 185, 196

Astor, John Jacob, 44, 46, 55

Astor Library, 55

Atlanta University, 88

Auburn, N.Y., 64

Augustus, John, 65

Australia, 170

Bahama Islands, 5

Baker, Newton D., 133

Baldwin Locomotive Co., 80

Baltimore, Md., 50, 55, 109, 115, 189

Bamberger, Louis, 195

Barlow et al. v. *A. P. Smith Manufacturing Co.*, 197

Barton, Clara, 125, 192; characterized, 92; in Civil War, 78; as Red Cross leader, 94–95; and Red Cross movement, 91–93

Bates, Joshua, 55

Beekman, James, 49

Belguim, relief of, in World War I, 126–28

Bellows, Henry W., 77, 80, 83, 91–92

Benevolent associations, 47, 87, 88, 103

"Benevolent Empire," 47–48, 96

Benezet, Anthony, 67, 188; antiwar tracts of, 28–29; charitable activities of, 26–27; defends Indian rights, 29; struggle of, for Negro rights, 29–31

Bennett, James Gordon, 97

Bible, 13, 32, 33, 47, 79

Bible Society of the Confederacy, 79

Bickerdyke, "Mother" Mary Ann, 78

Bicknell, Ernest, 128

Index

Blind, the, 46, 96, 154; Foundation for, 156, 194; Howe and, 66; "talking books" for, 156
Blithedale Romance, The (Hawthorne), 65
Boardman, Mabel, 125
Bond, Dr. Thomas, 25, 188
Bonifacius (Mather), 12. See also *Essays To Do Good*
Boston, Mass., 14, 18, 24, 44, 54, 55, 56, 60, 63, 65, 189; Associated Charities of, 103; fires in, 26, 94, 188, 191; freedmen's aid societies in, 84–85; Jewish Charities of, 124, 192; Mather on charity in, 1, 14; philanthropy in, 45, 109; relief crisis of 1774–75 in, 26, 188
Boston House of Reformation, 63
Boston Prison Discipline Society, 65, 189
Boston Public Library, 55
Boston Tea Party, 26
Boudinot, Elias, 46, 48
Boy Scouts of America, 123, 193
Brace, Charles Loring, 63–64, 191
Bradford, William, 6
Bridgman, Laura, 66, 190
British Sanitary Commission, 80
British War Relief, 169
Brooks, Peter Chardon, 45
Broun, Heywood, 161
Brown, John, 73–74
Brussels, Belgium, 126
Buffalo Charity Organization Society, 98, 192
Bunker Hill Monument Association, 55
Bureau of Refugees, Freedmen, and Abandoned Land, 86. See also Freedmen's Bureau
Burrus, James and John, 138
Bush Hill, pesthouse on, 39, 40
Butler, Cyrus, 46

Calhoun, John C., 53
California, 77

Campfire Girls, 123, 193
Canada, 68, 74, 170
Cape Verde Islands, 56
Capital punishment, 35
Capone, Al, 143
CARE (Cooperative for American Remittances to Everywhere), 171, 172, 182, 196
Carey, Mathew, 47, 190
Carnegie, Andrew, 105, 111, 121, 151, 193; benefactions of, 120, 194; and foundations, 117, 120–21; and gospel of wealth, 106–8, 114; on methods and objects of philanthropy, 108–10
Carnegie Corporation of New York, 117, 137, 138, 155, 156, 193
Carnegie Endowment for International Peace, 197
Carnegie Foundation for the Advancement of Teaching, 117, 120, 193
Carnegie Institution of Washington, 193
Catholic Protectory, 191
"Caution and Warning to Great Britain and Her Colonies, A" (Benezet), 30–31
C.C.C. (Civilian Conservation Corps), 163
Center for Advanced Study in the Behavioral Sciences, 178
Chamber of Commerce of the United States, 152
Channing, William Ellery, 47, 57, 67
Charitable deductions. See Taxation
Charity, 3, 4, 16, 61, 90, 94, 98, 116, 151, 154, 155, 174, 186; in depression of 1873–78, 96–97; in depression of 1930's, 143–51 *passim;* Ford on, 158; Hoover's view of, 144, 150–51; Mather on, 13–15; President Pierce on, 70; reform of, 60–62; Winthrop on, 7–8

Index

Charity organization movement and societies, 98–99, 102–3, 123, 124; motto of, 179–80; paid agents and caseworkers in, 97, 102–3; program of, 99–100, 102–3; volunteer workers in, 99–100, 102

Charity reformers, 47, 60–62, 90, 91, 103, 106, 108; in depression of 1873–78, 97–98

Charleston, S.C.: Brown Fellowship Society of, 189; fire in, 24; St. Andrew's Society of, 188

Chase, Stuart, 150

Cherry Hill, Penn., Eastern State Penitentiary at, 64

Chicago, Ill., 156; fire of 1871, 94, 191; Juvenile Court in, 192

Chicago, University of, 111, 117, 157

Child welfare, 61, 63–64, 96

Children's Bureau, U.S., 193

China, 167

Christ, Jesus, 22, 107

Christian Century, 161

Christian Commission, 79–80, 81, 84, 91

Churches: as objects of philanthropy, 45; and technical assistance program, 182–83

Cincinnati, Ohio, 85, 109

Civil War, 75, 89, 91, 93; nurses in, 77–78; philanthropy in, 76–88 *passim;* relief of servicemen in, 77–79; religious charities in, 79–80

Clarkson, Matthew, 38

Clarkson, Thomas, 31

Cleveland, Ohio, and community chest, 124, 193

Cleveland Foundation, 193

Cloisters, The, 157

Coffin, Levi, 74

Cold War, 174, 183

Colleges, 51–52, 86, 88

Colombia, 182

Colonization, philanthropic motives in, 7

Columbus, Christopher, 5

Columbus, Ohio, 112

Committee for Impartial Relief in Spain, 166

Commission for Relief in Belgium, 126–28, 193

Commission on Training Camp Activities, 131, 132

Common Sense (Paine), 34

Commonwealth Fund, 194

Community Chests, 134, 140–41, 159, 163, 169, 170, 194; in depression of 1930's, 144–48

Confederate States of America, war relief in, 78–79, 84

Congregational Board of Foreign Missions, 113

Congregationalists, 51

Congress of the United States, 53, 54, 66, 69, 70, 86, 118, 119, 145, 156, 167, 184, 193, 196; and hearings on unemployment relief, 148–49; and investigations of foundations, 175–76

Constitution of the United States, 70, 177

Continental Congress, 34

Cooper, Peter, 54, 191

Cooper Union, 54, 108, 191

Corporations, contributions to philanthropy, 173, 197

Cox Committee. *See* Select (Cox) Committee

CRALOG (Council of Relief Agencies Licensed to Operate in Germany), 171

Crimean War, 80

Crystal Palace Exhibition, 55

Curtis, Dr. Joseph, 44

Daily Graphic (N.Y.), 97

Dana, Richard Henry, 72

Dartmouth College, 23, 25, 46

Dartmouth College Case, 189

Davies, Joseph E., 169

Davis, Jefferson, 76

Davison, Henry P., 130, 131

Day, Clarence, quoted, 1

Index

Deaf, the, 69, 96; Gallaudet and, 66
Dearborn, Mich., 158
Declaration of Independence, 34, 177
Delavan, Edward, 58
Democracy, philanthropy and, 2, 57, 116
Democracy in America (Tocqueville), 42, 106, 190
Denver, Colo., 124, 192
Depression, 24; of 1816–21, 60; of 1837, 52; of 1873–78, 96–97; of 1930's, 141, 154
Detroit, Mich., 196
Development Loan Fund, 181
Devèze, Jean, 39, 40
Devine, Edward T., 115, 120
Dix, Dorothea, 65, 190; and care of the insane, 66, 67–70, 73; and Civil War nursing, 77; and public lands bill, 191
Do-goodism, 2, 181; Franklin and, 15, 17; influence of Great Awakening on, 21; Mather and, 12–14; Penn and, 11
Dogood, Silence, 15
Doles, 143, 150
Douglas, Paul, 150
Dreiser, Theodore, 150
Duke, James B., 138
Duke University, 138
Dunfermline, Scotland, 105
Dwight, Louis, 65, 189

East Cambridge, Mass., 67
Eastman, George, 138
Economic and Social History of the World War (Shotwell), 129, 139
Eddy, Thomas, 62
Education, 4, 35, 36, 46, 50–51, 69, 72; foundations and, 135–39; Freedmen's Bureau and, 87–88; General Education Board and, 120; of Indians, 25–26, 109; medical, 136; of Negroes, 86–88, 109,

110, 137–38; as object of philanthropy, 51–52, 110; and public school movement, 71–73, 137; Rush and, 35; southern, 88, 137–38
Edwards, Jonathan, 20, 21
Elect, doctrine of, 11
Eliot, John, 187
Emancipation Proclamation, 83
Embree, Edwin R., 176–77
Emerson, Ralph Waldo, 112; on philanthropy, 59; quoted, 58; on trade, 44
Encyclopedia of the Social Sciences, 139
England, 7, 23, 51, 61
Epidemics, 24; influenza (1918), 133; yellow fever, 36–40
Epstein, Abraham, 150
Essays To Do Good (Mather), 12–15, 188; influence of, on Franklin, 15
European Recovery Program, 172
European Relief Council, 134
Evangelical Tract Society, 79

Fairbanks, Calvin, 74
FERA (Federal Emergency Relief Administration), 195
Filene, Edward A., 194
Finland, 167
Fisk University, 88, 191; Jubilee Singers of, 110, 192
Flexner, Abraham, 120; contributions of, to medical education, 136
Folger, Henry C., 195
Folger Shakespeare Library, 195
Fontainebleau, restoration of, 139
Ford, Edsel, 160
Ford, Henry, 160, 177; on charity, 158
Ford Foundation, 160, 177, 179, 182, 195, 197; program and grants of, 178–79
Ford Motor Company, 146
Ford Museum, 158

Index

Foreign aid, 4, 56, 173, 181, 183; as economic and technical assistance, 181–85; as military assistance, 183–84. *See also* European Recovery Program; Overseas relief; Point Four Program
Fort Sumter, 77
Fortress Monroe, 84
Fortune, 177
Fosdick, Raymond, 132
Foundations, philanthropic, 117–21; contributions of, to education and research, 135–39; contributions of, to southern education, 137; investigations of, 119, 174–76, 177, 196, 197; Lindeman on, 160–61; number of, 139, 175; "scatteration" of, 156, 176; and taxation, 159–60, 174–75, 196; views on, in 1950's, 176–77
France, 38, 127, 167
Francke, August Hermann, 12, 22
Franco-Prussian War, 93
Franklin, Benjamin, 11, 54, 72, 90, 185, 188, 189; antislavery views of, 31; attitude of, toward charity and poor laws, 17–18; influences on career of, 15–16; philanthropic and civic activities of, 16–19; quoted on foreign aid, 165; social views of, 16; will of, 18
Franklin, James, 15
Franklin Funds, 189
Frauds, charitable, 180
Frederick the Great, 27, 28
Freedmen's aid associations, 84–88
Freedmen's Bureau, 191; activities of, 86–88; relations with freedmen's aid associations, 86–88
Freedmen's Inquiry Commission, 85
French and Indian War, 26
French West Indies, 38
Friendly Societies, 25
"Friendly Visiting," 99–100
Friends, Society of, 11, 15, 29–30. *See also* Quakers

Fugitive Slave Law, 73, 74, 75
Fuld, Mrs. Felix, 195
Full Employment Act (1946), 196
Fund for Adult Education, 178
Fund for the Advancement of Education, 178
Fund for the Republic, 178
Fund-raising, 132, 163, 166, 171; for Bunker Hill and Washington Monuments, 55–56; in Civil War, 77, 78–79, 82–84; by European Relief Council (1920–21), 134; and federated financing and community chest movement, 47, 124, 140–41, 192, 193, 194; for Greek relief, 56, 84; by Harvard endowment fund drive (1919), 138, 194; and health organizations, 180–81; for Irish famine relief, 56–57, 84; by President's Organization for Unemployment Relief (1931), 146–48, 195; profession of, 140; Red Cross war drives for (1917, 1918), 130–31, 194; for relief of Boston (1774–75), 26; by United Fund, 180, 196; by United War Work Fund (1918), 133; Whitefield and, 22–23; in World War II, 169–70; by "Y" drives, 124–25

Gallaudet, Thomas Hopkins, 66, 70, 189
Garrett, Thomas, 75
Garrison, William Lloyd, 49, 50
Gates, Frederick T., 112, 118, 192
General Education Board, 117, 119, 120, 136, 138, 155, 193
General Motors Corporation, 146
Geneva Convention of 1864, 92, 93, 192
Georgia, 23
German Pietists, 12
Germany, 126, 196
Gettysburg, battle of, 78
Gettysburg address, 83
Gifford, Walter S., 146, 148

Index

Gilded Age, 89

Gilman, Daniel Coit, quoted, 89

Girard, Stephen, 45, 58, 95, 190; on American doctors, 40; will of, 40–41; and yellow fever epidemic of 1793, 38–40

Girard College, 41, 191

Girl Scouts, 123, 193

Gladden, Washington, and "tainted money" controversy, 112–13, 192

Gladstone, William E., 106

God, 13, 45, 79, 106, 111; Franklin on, 17; Lawrence and, 45; Mather on, 13; Penn on, 10–11; Puritans covenant with, 7–8; Rockefeller and, 111–12; Winthrop on, 8

Goodwill Industries, 123

Gorki, Maxim, 135

Gospel of wealth. *See* Wealth, gospel of

Grand Tetons, 157

Gray, Francis, 54

Great Awakening, 20–22, 23, 24, 31, 188; influence of, on philanthropy, 21

Great Britain, 167

Great Depression. *See* Depression, of 1930's

Greece, 182

Greek War for Independence, 189; relief in, 56, 66

Greenfield Village, 158

Grinnell, Henry, 55

Griscom, John, 60, 62

Guggenheim, John Simon, Memorial Foundation, 194

Halle, Germany, 12, 23

Hampton Institute, 110, 191

Harkness, Edward S., 138; philanthropic activities of, 157, 195

Harpers Ferry, W. Va., 74

Harris, Elisha, 80

Harris, Seymour, 177

Hartley, Robert M., 61, 190

Harvard, John, 187

Harvard University, 12, 23, 44, 52, 54, 73, 109, 138, 157, 194, 195

Hawthorne, Nathaniel, 65

Health organizations, 180

Hebrew Sheltering and Immigrant Aid Society, 192

Helm, Peter, 39

Henry, Joseph, 53

Hill, Octavia, quoted, 100

History of the Standard Oil Company (Tarbell), 118

Hong Kong, 182

Hookworm disease, 136

Hoover, Herbert, 152, 194; on charity, 144, 150–51; and C.R.B., 126–28; and Great Depression, 144–51 *passim;* and overseas relief after World War I, 134–35, 194

Hopkins, Mark, 53

Hopper, Isaac, 65

Hospital Sketches (Alcott), 78

Hospitals, 67, 69, 86; in Civil War, 81–82; as objects of philanthropy, 45, 90. *See also* Pennsylvania Hospital

House of industry, 62; *See also* Almshouse

How Tax Laws Make Giving to Charity Easy (Lasser), 173

Howard, John, 36

Howard, Major General Oliver O., 86, 88

Howard University, 88

Howe, Samuel Gridley, 65, 66, 68, 70, 72, 95, 189, 190; in abolition movement, 73; and education of the blind, 66; and Freedmen's Inquiry Commission, 85; as member of U.S. Sanitary Commission, 81

Hull House, 113, 192

Humanitarian reform, 3, 4; Benezet and, 27–31; in pre–Civil War period, 59–75 *passim*

Humanities, philanthropic support of, 156

Index

Illinois, 193
Index of American Design, 162
India, 182, 189
Indians, 27; Benezet's interest in, 29; as earliest American philanthropists, 5; missionary and educational work among, 25, 187; as objects of philanthropy, 7, 109
Insane, the: B. Rush and treatment of, 34; Dorothea Dix and treatment of, 66, 67–70, 73. *See also* Mentally ill, the
Institute for Advanced Study, 195
International Committee of the Red Cross, 93
International Health Commission, 136
Iowa, 77
Irish famine relief (1846–47), 56–57, 190
Israel, aid to, 173, 196
Italy, 68, 182

Japan, 69
Jernegan, Marcus W., 141
Jewish Welfare Board, 132
Jews, 81, 166, 172, 173
Johnson, Andrew, 86
Johnstown flood, 94
Junto, 18, 188
Juvenile delinquency, 62–64

Kansas, 73, 74
Kansas-Nebraska Act, 73
Keller, Helen, 192, 194
Kellogg Foundation, 157, 195
Kentucky, 74
Kenyon College, 52
King, Thomas Starr, 84
King Philip's War, 187
Knights of Columbus, 132
Korean War, 183

"Lady Bountiful of the Bowery," 144
LARA (Licensed Agencies for Relief in Asia), 171

Lasser, J. K., 173
Laurens, Henry, 28
Lawrence, Abbott, 44, 52, 54, 73, 191
Lawrence, Amos, 44, 45, 46, 53, 55, 58, 101, 111, 159, 190
Lawrence, Amos Adams, 73
Lawrenceville School, 157
Lee, Ivy, 118
Liberia, 48, 49
Liberty Loan, 131
Libraries: Carnegie and, 110; as objects of philanthropy, 55, 110
Library of Congress, 139, 156
Lighthouse, the, 123
Lincoln, Abraham, 76, 77, 79, 81, 83, 85, 86
Lindeman, Eduard C., 160–61
London, England, 32, 55, 126
London Charity Organization Society, 98, 191
Louis, Jean, 188
Lowell, John, 54, 190
Lowell, Josephine Shaw, 95, 98; philanthropic views and activities of, 100–3
Lowell, Mass., 44
Lowell Institute, 54, 190
Lyman, Theodore, 45–46, 63

McDonogh, John, 49
McDowell, Mary, 115
McKaye, James, 85
McLean, John, 67
McMain, Eleanor, 115
Madeira Islands, 56
Magnalia Christi Americana (Mather), 187
Mann, Horace, 43, 65, 190; in antislavery movement, 73; educational reforms of, 70–73
March of Dimes, 163, 197
Marshall Plan, 172
Maryland, 49
Masonic order, 40
Massachusetts, 12, 24, 49, 57, 68, 73, 78; Board of State Charities in, 95; legislature of, 54; State

222

Index

Board of Education in, 72, 73; state reformatory in, 46

Massachusetts General Hospital, 109, 189

Mather, Cotton, 15, 16, 17, 63, 90, 101, 134, 151, 187, 188; attitude of, toward charity, 13–15; on charity in Boston, 1, 14–15; and doctrine of stewardship, 13; on doing good, 5, 13; philanthropic principles of, 12–15

Mather, Samuel, 15

Medical Bureau, U.S. Army, 77, 81

Medical Education in the United States and Canada (Flexner), 120

Mellon, Andrew W., 161–62, 195

Mellon, A. W., Charitable and Educational Trust, 157, 162

Memoirs of Herbert Hoover, 147

Memorial to the Legislature of Massachusetts (Dix), 68, 69, 190

Mentally ill, the, 67, 69. *See also,* Insane, the

Metropolitan Museum of Art, 157

Metropolitan Opera Company, 155

Mexico, 182

Middle East, 54, 182

"Millionaire class," 106, 109

Mission and tract societies, 48

Missionaries, 182, 187, 189

Missouri, 193

"Model of Christian Charity, A" (Winthrop), 7–8, 187

Moody, Dwight L., 124

Moral reform, 47, 50, 58

Morgan, J. P., 123

Morgan, J. P., and Co., 130

Morristown, N.J., 45

"Mothers' Pension" laws, 193

Mott, John R., 133

Mt. Desert Island, 157

Muckraking, 117

Murphy, J. Prentice, 149

Mutual Security Act, 1957, 181

Nashville, Tenn., 138

Nation, 161

National Association for the Advancement of Colored People, 123

National Bureau of Economic Research, 156

National Catholic Community Service, 168

National Child Labor Committee, 123

National Conference of Charities and Correction, 95, 112, 191

National Conference on Social Welfare, 191

National Foundation. *See* National Foundation for Infantile Paralysis

National Foundation for Infantile Paralysis, 163, 180, 196, 197

National Gallery of Art, 162, 195

National Jewish Welfare Board, 168

National Merit Scholarship Corporation, 178, 197

National Travelers Aid Association, 168

National Tuberculosis Association, 119, 123, 155, 193

National Urban League, 123

National War Fund, Inc., 169–70, 196

Negroes: Benezet's interest in, 29–31; in Civil War, 84–85; foundations and education of, 86–88, 137–38; free, 31, 48, 49, 50; and freedmen's aid associations, 84–85; and Freedmen's Bureau, 86–88; as fugitive slaves, 74–75; higher education for, 88, 110, 138. *See also* Slavery

Neutrality Act of 1939, 166–67, 196

New Deal: and philanthropy, 154–55, 158–59, 162–63; relief and security programs of, 153–54

New England, 6, 7, 9, 22, 26, 44, 56, 77; hurricane of 1938, 163

New Jersey, 26, 95

New Orleans, La., 55; Charity

New Orleans, La. (*continued*)
Hospital in, 188; orphanage at Ursuline Convent in, 188
New Republic, 161
New York (City), 45, 54, 56, 60, 62, 63, 80, 84, 85, 91, 98, 109, 140, 157
New York (State), 61, 62, 64, 77, 95, 119, 151, 152; State Board of Charity in, 103
New York Association for Improving the Condition of the Poor, 61, 190
New York Charity Organization Society, 98, 115, 146
New York Children's Aid Society, 63–64, 191
New York House of Refuge, 62, 189
New York Philharmonic Orchestra, 155
New York School of Philanthropy, 192
New York Society for the Prevention of Pauperism, 62, 189
New York Times Company, 139
New Zealand, 127, 170
Niebuhr, Reinhold, quoted, 143
Noguchi, Hideyo, 136
North American Review, 105
North Oxford, Mass., 92
Northampton, Mass., 45

Oberlin College, 52
Ogden, Robert C., 88
Oglethorpe, James, 188
Old-age insurance, 150. *See also* Social insurance
Olmsted, Frederick Law, 81, 83
Olyphant, David, 48
Orphanages, 86, 90, 96; Francke's and Whitefield's, 22–23; as objects of philanthropy, 45
Outdoor relief, 97–98. *See also* Poor relief
Overseas relief: to China, 166; to Greece, 56, 66; in Irish famine, 56–57, 190; in Russian famine,

135, 194; in Spanish Civil War, 166; in World War I (1914–17), 125–29, 193; after World War I, 134–35; in World War II, 165–71; since World War II, 171–72, 181–85. *See also* Foreign aid; War relief
Owen, Robert, 189
Owen, Robert Dale, 85

Page, Walter Hines, 126
Paine, Robert Treat, 89; quoted, 103–4
Paine, Thomas, 34
Panic of 1837, 48. *See also* Depression of 1837
Paris, France, and World's Fair of 1867, 84
Parker, Theodore, 66, 74
Pauperism, 102, 103, 108, 116; fear of, 60, 94, 97–98, 100
Paupers, care of, 61–62, 103
Peabody, George, 55, 88, 191
Peabody Fund, 191
Peabody Institute (Baltimore), 55
Pearl Harbor, 168
Penn, William, 9, 12, 16, 106, 187; and doctrine of stewardship, 10; on doing good, 11; social views of, 9–11
Pennsylvania, 9, 26, 27, 35, 40, 41, 45; gradual emancipation act in, 31, 188; prison system in, 64–65
Pennsylvania, University of, 18, 23
Pennsylvania Hospital, 18, 25, 41, 188
Pennsylvania Society for Promoting the Abolition of Slavery, 31
Perkins, Thomas H., 46
Perkins Institution, 66, 190
Persia, 129
Philadelphia, 18, 26, 27, 29, 32, 40, 45, 56, 64, 84, 85, 98, 115, 149; House of Refuge in, 62–63; philanthropy in, 109; yellow fever epidemics in, 36–39, 40, 189

Index

Philadelphia Bettering House, 25, 188

Philadelphia Dispensary, 34, 35

Philadelphia Inquirer, 141

"Philanthropology," 90

Philanthropy: Aim and functions of, 2–3, 154–55; American attitudes toward, 1, 2, 45, 120, 141, 145–50, 159, 160–61, 185–86; atonement theory of, 44–45; and charity, 3; in colonial period, 24–26; "dead hand" in, 191; and democracy, 2, 57, 116; European backgrounds of American, 6–7; and foundations, 120–21; founders of American, 7; and gospel of wealth, 107–8; influence of Great Awakening on, 21; motives of, 3, 45, 118; and Negro and southern education, 88, 137–38; and New Deal, 154, 158–59; objects of, 3–4, 45–46, 51–52, 55, 90, 109–10; and overseas aid (1939–45), 172; program of, in 1950's, 179–80; and public relations, 118; and reform, 3, 4, 59–61, 71, 104; "retail," 122–23; Rush and Girard as representative of trends in American, 41; scientific, 17, 89–104 *passim,* 115, 184; sources of, 139–40, 179; as subject of research, 4; and taxation, 97–98, 133, 159–60, 173–74; and the technical assistance program, 182–83; tendency of, in U.S., 17, 151; training courses in, 115; "wholesale," 112, 116; World War I influence on, 129–40 *passim*

Phillips Exeter Academy, 157, 195

Phrenology, 72

Pierce, Franklin, 69–70, 191

Pilgrim's Progress (Bunyan), 35

Pittsburgh Survey, 119

Pius IX, 84

Plymouth, Mass., 6

Point Four Program, 181–82, 183–84, 196

Poland, 129, 165

Poor, the, 3, 14, 16, 17, 25, 70, 97, 143, 180; and charity reformers, 60–61; Franklin on, 17–18; "friendly visiting" of, 99–100; Mrs. Lowell on, 101; Mather on, 14–15; Whitefield's concern for, 22

Poor relief, 16, 17, 23–24, 79, 148, 154; criticism of, 61, 97–98; Elizabethan Poor Law (1601), 187; in England, 7, 61

Poor Richard's Almanack (Franklin), 16

Poughkeepsie, N.Y., 61

Poverty, 17, 72, 100, 116; in underdeveloped or overexploited areas, 181–85

Pratt, Enoch, 110

Pratt Free Library (Baltimore), 110

Pratt Institute (Brooklyn), 108

President's Birthday Balls, 163, 195

President's Committee on War Relief Agencies, 168

President's Organization for Unemployment Relief, fund appeal (1931), 146–48, 195

President's War Relief Control Board, 168–69, 182, 196

Princeton University, 23, 32

Prison reform, 35, 64–65, 91

Prisons and reformatories, 42, 64–65; institutions for juveniles, 62–63, 64, 73

Progressive era, 115

Prohibition amendment, 133

Protestant Church World Service, 172

Providence, R.I., 74

Public Administration Clearing House, 156

Public health movement, 91

Public land, 69, 70

Public welfare, 70, 95–96; before Great Depression, 141; during Great Depression, 152–54

Puritans, 7, 9, 187

Index

Quakers, 9–12, 27, 75. *See also* Friends, Society of
Quincy, Josiah, 57, 63

Randolph, John, 49
Reconstruction, 86, 88
Reconstruction Finance Corporation, 152, 195
Red Cross movement, 92–93. *See also* American National Red Cross
Reece, B. Carroll, 177
Reece Committee. *See* Special (Reece) Committee
Reform. *See* Humanitarian reform; Moral reform; Social reform
Relief. *See* Poor relief; Unemployment, relief of; War relief
Relief and aid organization, 47
Religion, 4. *See also* Churches; Do-goodism; God; Stewardship, doctrine of
Remarks on Prisons and Prison Discipline (Dix), 65, 190
Resources for the Future, 178
Review of Reviews, 109
Rheims Cathedral, restoration of, 139
Rhodes Scholars, 127
Richmond, Mary E., 115, 194
Rockefeller, John D., 123, 136, 151; benefactions of, 111, 120, 192, 193, 195; and the doctrine of stewardship, 111–12; and philanthropic foundations, 116–21; quoted, on philanthropic trusts, 105, 117; and "tainted money" controversy, 112–13, 118
Rockefeller, John D., Jr., 133, 139, 157, 194; benefaction of, 157, 196
Rockefeller, Laura Spelman, Memorial, 135
Rockefeller Foundation, 117, 120, 138, 176, 182, 193, 195; controversy over incorporation of, 118–19; and medical research and education, 135–36; program

changes of, in 1930's, 156–57; and U.S. Industrial Relations Commission, 119; war relief activities of, in World War I, 128
Rockefeller Institute for Medical Research, 117, 192
Rockefeller Sanitary Commission, 120, 128
Roman Catholic War Relief Services, 172
Roman Catholics, 64; nuns, 77, 143, 188, 189; Society of St. Vincent de Paul, 190
Roosevelt, Franklin D., 158, 168; attitudes of, toward charity, 151–52; and New Deal, 152–54; on relations between private and governmental welfare agencies, 163
Root, Elihu, 120
Rose, Wickliffe, 128
Rosenwald, Julius, 137
Rosenwald Funds, 155, 156, 176; contributions to Negro education, 137, 194
Rush, Benjamin, 27, 28, 31, 66, 95; on American Revolution, 33–34; on capital punishment, 35; on Girard, 39–40; on "Humane Mania," quoted, 20; medical views of, 33; as reformer, 31, 33–37, 41; religious views of, 31–33; and yellow fever epidemic of 1793, 36–39
Russell Sage Foundation, 115, 117, 119, 193
Russia, 129, 135, 167
Russian famine relief (1921–22), 135, 194
Russo-Turkish War, 93
Rutgers University, 52

Sabbath observance, 47
Sage, Russell, Foundation. *See* Russell Sage Foundation
Salk vaccine, 180, 197
Salvation Army, 123, 132, 168
San Francisco, Calif., 84

Index

Sanborn, Franklin B., 95
Sandusky, Ohio, 74
Sanitary Commission. *See* United States Sanitary Commission
Sanitary Fairs, 82–83, 191
Santo Domingo, 38
Saturday Evening Post, 141, 159
Schuyler, Louisa Lee, 81
Scientific research, as object of philanthropy, 54
Scotland, 68
Scots charitable Society, 187
Sea Islands, 85, 88; hurricane on, 94
Sears, Roebuck, and Company, 137, 155
Second Bank of the United States, 40
Select (Cox) Committee, 176–77, 196
Selective Service Act (1940), 167
Sentinels of the Republic, 152
Serbia, 129
Seton, Mother Elizabeth Bayley, 189
Settlement houses, 114–15, 123, 194
Shaler, Millard K., 126
Shattuck, George Cheyne, 46
Shaw, Albert, 110
Sherman Antitrust Act, 118
Shotwell, James T., 129
Silliman, Benjamin, 54
Simkhovitch, Mary Kingsbury, 115
Sisters of Charity of St. Joseph, 189
Slater, John F., 88; Fund, 192
Slavery, 6, 23, 29, 35, 48, 73, 74; ending of, 84
Slaves: fugitive, 74–75; manumission of, 49
Slave-trade, 27, 30–31, 33
Sloan Foundation, 157
Sloane, Rush R., 74
Smith, Gerrit, 73–74
Smith, John, 26, 28
Smithson, James, bequest of, 53–54

Smithsonian Institution, 53–54, 190
Social Diagnosis (Richmond), 115, 194
Social insurance, 153
Social reform, 115, 116, 120; and gospel of wealth, 107; in pre–Civil War period, 59–60; and scientific philanthropy, 104
Social Science Research Council, 139
Social sciences, philanthropic support of research in, 138–39, 156, 178
Social Security Act, 195
Social work, 115, 116, 120, 194
Social workers, 115–16; attitudes of, in depression of 1930's, 148–49
Society for Alleviating the Miseries of Public Prisons, 64
Society for Promoting Manual Training in Literary Institutions, 52
Society for Promoting the Observance of the Seventh Commandment, 50
Society for Promotion of Collegiate and Theological Education in the West, 52
Society for the Propagation of the Gospel in New England, 187
Society of St. Vincent de Paul, 190
Some Historical Account of Guinea (Benezet), 31
South America, 136
South Carolina, 23
Southern Baptist Convention, 135
Southern Education Board, 137, 138
Spanish Civil War, 166
Special (Reece) Committee, 176, 197
Spencer, Herbert, 107
Squanto, 5–6
Standard Oil of New Jersey, 118
Stanford, Leland, 110, 192
Stanford University, 192

Index

Stanton, Edwin M., 81, 86

State, U.S., Department of, 167

State boards of charity, personnel and activities of, 95–96

State Charities Aid Associations, 95

Statute of Charitable Uses (1601), 187

Sterling, John W., 138, 194

Stewardship, doctrine of, 45, 50, 73, 181; Benezet on, 28; contrasted with gospel of wealth, 106; and Lawrence, 45; Mann on, 72; Mather on, 13; Penn on, 10; Rockefeller on, 111–12

Stewart, A. T., 56, 83

Stock market crash (1929), 155

Straus, Jesse Isidore, 159

Sullivan, Anne, 192

Sumner, Charles, 65, 73

Sunday-school movement, 47

Supreme Court of the United States, 118, 154, 189

Survey, 115

Survey Graphic, 142

Switzerland, 93

Taft, Charles P., 169

Taft, William Howard, 118

"Tainted Money" (Gladden), 112

"Tainted Money" controversy, 112–13, 139, 192, 193

Tappan, Arthur, 48, 50, 190

Tappan, Lewis, 48, 50, 190

Tappans (Arthur and Lewis), the, 49–50, 52, 58, 87

Tarbell, Ida M., 117

Taxation, 25, 97, 185; charitable deductions authorized for corporations, 158, 195; and foundations, 159–60, 174–75, 196; income tax amendment of 1917, 133, 194; and philanthropy, 97–98, 133, 159–60, 173–74; Revenue Act of 1935, 159, 195

Technical Assistance, 181; voluntary agencies in, 182–83

Thoreau, Henry David: on charity, 59; on philanthropy, 44

Thoughts on the Nature of War (Benezet), 28

Thoughts on Slavery (Wesley), 31

Time, 146

Tobey, Senator Charles W., 174, 196

Tocqueville, Alexis de, 57, 106, 151, 190; on the rich in a democracy, 43; quoted on virtue in the United States, 42

Torrey, Charles, 74

Touro, Judah, 55

Toynbee Hall, 192

Tragic America (Dreiser), 150

Tribune (N.Y.), 109, 192

Tripp, Peter, 197

Truman, Harry S., and Point Four Program, 181–82, 183–84, 196

Tubman, Harriet, 74, 78

Tuckerman, Joseph, 60, 61, 90, 190

Turkey, 68, 129, 182

Tuskegee Institute, 110, 192

Twentieth Century Fund, 194

Two Years Before the Mast (Dana), 72

Underground railway, 74

Unemployment, 142, 153; relief of, in 1930's, 148, 151–52, 153, 195

Unemployment insurance, 150, 154

Unitarians, 190

United Fund, 180, 196

United Jewish Appeal, 169, 173, 196

United Nations agencies: Food and Agriculture Organization, 181; International Bank for Reconstruction and Development, 181–82; International Children's Fund, 181; World Health Organization, 181

United Nations Relief and Re-

Index

habilitation Administration (UNRRA), 170–71, 196
United Palestine Appeal, 173
United Service for New Americans, 173
United Service Organizations for National Defense (U.S.O.), 168, 169, 196
United Service to China, 169
United States Army, 172
United States Food Administration, 134
United States Grain Corporation, 134, 135
United States Industrial Relations Commission, 119, 194
United States International Cooperation Administration, 182
United States Sanitary Commission, 77, 91, 92, 95, 191; in Civil War, 80–84; fund-raising by, 82–84
United States Steel Corporation, 146
United War Work Fund, 1918, 133, 194

Valley Forge, 145
Van Rensselaer, Stephen, 48
Vanderbilt, Cornelius, 83
Veblen, Thorstein, 112
Versailles, restoration of, 139
Vincent, George E., 135; quoted, 122
Virginia, 49
Volga Relief Society, 135

Wald, Lillian, 115
War Camp Community Service, 132
War Department, U.S., 86
War of 1812, 40
War relief, 4; in Civil War, 76–80; in World War I, 125–35, 193; in World War II, 167–70
Ward, Charles S., 130
Warm Springs Foundation, 151
Warren, Charles, 169

Washington, D.C., 53, 195
Washington, Booker T., 137, 192
Washington, George, 34
Washington Monument, 55–56
Washington National Monument Society, 55
"Way to Wealth" (Franklin), 16
Wealth: American attitudes toward, 43–44; and education, 72–73; gospel of, 106–8; surplus, 59, 106–9, 122
"Wealth" (Carnegie), 105, 111, 192
Wealth and Culture (Lindeman), 160
Welfare. See Child welfare; Public welfare
Wesley, John, 31
West, Walter, 149
West Indies, 38
Westborough, Mass., reform school, 63, 73
Western Sanitary Commission, 83, 85
Wheelock, Eleazar, 25
White House Conference on the Care of Dependent Children (1909), 193
Whitefield, George, 21, 32, 41, 188; and Great Awakening, 21–22; and orphanage in Georgia, 22–23
Whitlock, Brand, 126
Whitman, Walt, quoted, 76
Whyte, William H., Jr., 176–77
Wickersham, George, 118
Williams, Roger, 9
Williams College, 53
Williamsburg, Va., restoration of, 139, 157, 194
Wilmington, Del., 75
Wilson, Woodrow, 126, 129
Wines, Frederick H., 95
Winthrop, John (1588–1649), 7–9, 10, 57, 106, 187; "A Model of Christian Charity," 7–9
Winthrop, John (1606–76), 9
Winthrop, Robert, 49, 57

Index

Wisconsin, University of, 139

Woolman, John, 29

Woolsey sisters, 77

Worcester (Mass.) Asylum, 68

World War I, 125, 131, 168; influence of, on American philanthropy, 129–40 *passim;* war relief in, 125–35

World War II, 129, 131; overseas aid and war relief activities in, 165–71

WPA (Works Progress Administration), 162, 163

Yale, Elihu, 188

Yale University, 12, 78, 138, 157, 194, 195

Yeatman, James, 85

Yellow fever epidemic (1793), 36–40, 189

Young Men's Christian Association, 79, 123, 130, 132, 133, 143, 168, 191; fund-raising drives of, 124–25

Young Men's Hebrew Association, 123

Young Women's Christian Association, 123, 132, 168

Zinsser, Hans, 136

23838